MznLnx

Missing Links Exam Preps

Exam Prep for

Management

Gomez-Mejia, Balkin, & Cardy, 3rd Edition

The MznLnx Exam Prep is your link from the texbook and lecture to your exams.
The MznLnx Exam Preps are unauthorized and comprehensive reviews of your textbooks.

All material provided by MznLnx and Rico Publications (c) 2010
Textbook publishers and textbook authors do not particpate in or contribute to these reviews.

MznLnx

Rico Publications

Exam Prep for Management
3rd Edition
Gomez-Mejia, Balkin, & Cardy

Publisher: Raymond Houge
Assistant Editor: Michael Rouger
Text and Cover Designer: Lisa Buckner
Marketing Manager: Sara Swagger
Project Manager, Editorial Production: Jerry Emerson
Art Director: Vernon Lowerui

Product Manager: Dave Mason
Editorial Asitant: Rachel Guzmanji
Pedagogy: Debra Long
Cover Image: Jim Reed/Getty Images
Text and Cover Printer: City Printing, Inc.
Compositor: Media Mix, Inc.

(c) 2010 Rico Publications

ALL RIGHTS RESERVED. No part of this work covered by the copyright may be reproduced or used in any form or by an means--graphic, electronic, or mechanical, including photocopying, recording, taping, Web distribution, information storage, and retrieval systems, or in any other manner--without the written permission of the publisher.

Printed in the United States
ISBN:

For more information about our products, contact us at:
Dave.Mason@RicoPublications.com

For permission to use material from this text or product, submit a request online to:
Dave.Mason@RicoPublications.com

Contents

CHAPTER 1
Management and Its Evolution — 1

CHAPTER 2
Managing in a Global Environment — 12

CHAPTER 3
Managing Social Responsibility and Ethics — 23

CHAPTER 4
Managing Organizational Culture and Change — 28

CHAPTER 5
Managing the Planning Process — 32

CHAPTER 6
Decision Making — 36

CHAPTER 7
Strategic Management — 41

CHAPTER 8
Entrepreneurship and Innovation — 48

CHAPTER 9
Managing the Structure and Design of Organizations — 55

CHAPTER 10
Human Resources Management — 61

CHAPTER 11
Managing Employee Diversity — 75

CHAPTER 12
Motivation — 82

CHAPTER 13
Leadership — 87

CHAPTER 14
Managing Teams — 90

CHAPTER 15
Managing Communication — 94

CHAPTER 16
Management Control — 97

CHAPTER 17
Operations Management — 100

CHAPTER 18
Managing Information System — 106

ANSWER KEY — 114

TO THE STUDENT

COMPREHENSIVE

The *MznLnx* Exam Prep series is designed to help you pass your exams. Editors at MznLnx review your textbooks and then prepare these practice exams to help you master the textbook material. Unlike study guides, workbooks, and practice tests provided by the texbook publisher and textbook authors, *MznLnx* gives you **all** of the material in each chapter in exam form, not just samples, so you can be sure to nail your exam.

MECHANICAL

The MznLnx Exam Prep series creates exams that will help you learn the subject matter as well as test you on your understanding. Each question is designed to help you master the concept. Just working through the exams, you gain an understanding of the subject--its a simple mechanical process that produces success.

INTEGRATED STUDY GUIDE AND REVIEW

MznLnx is not just a set of exams designed to test you, its also a comprehensive review of the subject content. Each exam question is also a review of the concept, making sure that you will get the answer correct without having to go to other sources of material. You learn as you go! Its the easiest way to pass an exam.

HUMOR

Studying can be tedious and dry. MznLnx's instructional design includes moderate humor within the exam questions on occassion, to break the tedium and revitalize the brain

Chapter 1. Management and Its Evolution 1

1. _____ is a form of applied ethics that examines ethical principles and moral or ethical problems that arise in a business environment. It applies to all aspects of business conduct and is relevant to the conduct of individuals and business organizations as a whole. Applied ethics is a field of ethics that deals with ethical questions in many fields such as medical, technical, legal and _____.

   a. Hypernorms
   b. Corporate Sustainability
   c. Facilitation payments
   d. Business ethics

2. _____ is the provision of service to customers before, during and after a purchase.

   According to Turban et al. (2002), '_____ is a series of activities designed to enhance the level of customer satisfaction - that is, the feeling that a product or service has met the customer expectation.'

   Its importance varies by product, industry and customer; defective or broken merchandise can be exchanged, often only with a receipt and within a specified time frame.

   a. Service rate
   b. 28-hour day
   c. 1990 Clean Air Act
   d. Customer service

3. _____ in its literal sense is the process of transformation of local or regional phenomena into global ones. It can be described as a process by which the people of the world are unified into a single society and function together.

   This process is a combination of economic, technological, sociocultural and political forces.

   a. Collaborative Planning, Forecasting and Replenishment
   b. Histogram
   c. Globalization
   d. Cost Management

4. _____ is subcontracting a process, such as product design or manufacturing, to a third-party company. The decision to outsource is often made in the interest of lowering cost or making better use of time and energy costs, redirecting or conserving energy directed at the competencies of a particular business, or to make more efficient use of land, labor, capital, (information) technology and resources. _____ became part of the business lexicon during the 1980s.

   a. Operant conditioning
   b. Unemployment insurance
   c. Opinion leadership
   d. Outsourcing

5. _____ is an advertisement in which a particular product specifically mentions a competitor by name for the express purpose of showing why the competitor is inferior to the product naming it.

   This should not be confused with parody advertisements, where a fictional product is being advertised for the purpose of poking fun at the particular advertisement, nor should it be confused with the use of a coined brand name for the purpose of comparing the product without actually naming an actual competitor. ('Wikipedia tastes better and is less filling than the Encyclopedia Galactica.')

   In the 1980s, during what has been referred to as the cola wars, soft-drink manufacturer Pepsi ran a series of advertisements where people, caught on hidden camera, in a blind taste test, chose Pepsi over rival Coca-Cola.

a. 1990 Clean Air Act	b. 28-hour day
c. Comparative advertising	d. 33 Strategies of War

6. The term '_____' refers to the concept of collecting information and attempting to spot a pattern in the information. In some fields of study, the term '_____' has more formally-defined meanings.

In project management _____ is a mathematical technique that uses historical results to predict future outcome.

a. Regression analysis	b. Least squares
c. Stepwise regression	d. Trend analysis

7.

The terms _____ and positive action refer to policies that take race, ethnicity, or gender into consideration in an attempt to promote equal opportunity. The focus of such policies ranges from employment and education to public contracting and health programs. The impetus towards _____ is twofold: to maximize diversity in all levels of society, along with its presumed benefits, and to redress perceived disadvantages due to overt, institutional, or involuntary discrimination.

a. Affirmative action	b. Affiliation
c. Abraham Harold Maslow	d. Adam Smith

8. A _____ is a name or trademark connected with a product or producer. _____s have become increasingly important components of culture and the economy, now being described as 'cultural accessories and personal philosophies'.

Some people distinguish the psychological aspect of a _____ from the experiential aspect.

a. Brand	b. Brand extension
c. Brand loyalty	d. Brand awareness

9. _____ refers to increasing the spiritual, political, social or economic strength of individuals and communities. It often involves the empowered developing confidence in their own capacities.

The term Human _____ covers a vast landscape of meanings, interpretations, definitions and disciplines ranging from psychology and philosophy to the highly commercialized Self-Help industry and Motivational sciences.

a. A Stake in the Outcome	b. A4e
c. AAAI	d. Empowerment

Chapter 1. Management and Its Evolution

10. _____ has been described as the 'process of social influence in which one person can enlist the aid and support of others in the accomplishment of a common task'. A definition more inclusive of followers comes from Alan Keith of Genentech who said '_____ is ultimately about creating a way for people to contribute to making something extraordinary happen.'

_____ is one of the most salient aspects of the organizational context. However, defining _____ has been challenging.

a. 1990 Clean Air Act
b. Leadership
c. 28-hour day
d. Situational leadership

11. Procter is a surname, and may also refer to:

- Bryan Waller Procter (pseud. Barry Cornwall), English poet
- Goodwin Procter, American law firm
- _____, consumer products multinational

a. Master and Servant Acts
b. Strict liability
c. Downstream
d. Procter ' Gamble

12. A _____ is a group of employees from various functional areas of the organization - research, engineering, marketing, finance. human resources, and operations, for example - who are all focused on a specific objective and are responsible to work as a team to improve coordination and innovation across divisions and resolve mutual problems.

a. Sociotechnical systems
b. Graduate recruitment
c. Goal-setting theory
d. Cross-functional team

13. A _____ is a list of the general tasks and responsibilities of a position. Typically, it also includes to whom the position reports, specifications such as the qualifications needed by the person in the job, salary range for the position, etc. A _____ is usually developed by conducting a job analysis, which includes examining the tasks and sequences of tasks necessary to perform the job.

a. Recruitment
b. Recruitment Process Insourcing
c. Recruitment advertising
d. Job description

14. _____ is a strategic planning method used to evaluate the Strengths, Weaknesses, Opportunities, and Threats involved in a project or in a business venture. It involves specifying the objective of the business venture or project and identifying the internal and external factors that are favorable and unfavorable to achieving that objective. The technique is credited to Albert Humphrey, who led a convention at Stanford University in the 1960s and 1970s using data from Fortune 500 companies.

a. Market share
b. Corporate image
c. Marketing
d. SWOT analysis

15. In politics, a _____, (by metaphor with the carved _____ at the prow of a sailing ship), is a person who holds an important title or office yet executes little actual power, most commonly limited by convention rather than law. Common _____s include constitutional monarchs, such as: Queen Elizabeth II, the Emperor of Japan, or presidents in parliamentary democracies, such as the President of Israel.

While the authority of a _____ is in practice generally symbolic, public opinion, respect for the office or the office holder and access to high levels of government can give them significant influence on events.

   a. 33 Strategies of War
   b. 28-hour day
   c. 1990 Clean Air Act
   d. Figurehead

16. _____ is a class of behavioural theory that claims that there is no best way to organize a corporation, to lead a company, or to make decisions. Instead, the optimal course of action is contingent (dependant) upon the internal and external situation. Several contingency approaches were developed concurrently in the late 1960s.
   a. Contingency theory
   b. Distributed management
   c. Commercial management
   d. Capability management

17. An _____ is a person who has possession of an enterprise and assumes significant accountability for the inherent risks and the outcome. It is an ambitious leader who combines land, labor, and capital to create and market new goods or services. The term is a loanword from French and was first defined by the Irish economist Richard Cantillon.
   a. A4e
   b. A Stake in the Outcome
   c. Entrepreneur
   d. AAAI

18. A _____ is the term given to a company that facilitates the learning of its members and continuously transforms itself. _____s develop as a result of the pressures facing modern organizations and enables them to remain competitive in the business environment. A _____ has five main features; systems thinking, personal mastery, mental models, shared vision and team learning.
   a. Hoshin Kanri
   b. 1990 Clean Air Act
   c. Quality function deployment
   d. Learning organization

19. _____ is used to assign the available resources in an economic way. It is part of resource management.

In strategic planning,is a plan for using available resources, for example human resources, especially in the near term, to achieve goals for the future.

   a. 28-hour day
   b. 1990 Clean Air Act
   c. 33 Strategies of War
   d. Resource allocation

20. _____ is an interdisciplinary field of science and the study of the nature of complex systems in nature, society, and science. More specifically, it is a framework by which one can analyze and/or describe any group of objects that work in concert to produce some result. This could be a single organism, any organization or society, or any electro-mechanical or informational artifact.
   a. 28-hour day
   b. 1990 Clean Air Act
   c. Systems thinking
   d. Systems theory

21. _____ is a term defined by the Oxford English Dictionary as an individual's 'course or progress through life '. It is usually considered to pertain to remunerative work (and sometimes also formal education.)

The etymology of the term is somewhat ironic in that it comes from the Latin word carrera, which means race .

a. Career planning
c. Nursing shortage
b. Spatial mismatch
d. Career

22. _____ was a Scottish moral philosopher and a pioneer of political economy. One of the key figures of the Scottish Enlightenment, Smith is the author of The Theory of Moral Sentiments and An Inquiry into the Nature and Causes of the Wealth of Nations. The latter, usually abbreviated as The Wealth of Nations, is considered his magnum opus and the first modern work of economics.
   a. Adam Smith
   c. Affirmative action
   b. Abraham Harold Maslow
   d. Affiliation

23. _____ is an area of business concerned with the production of goods and services, and involves the responsibility of ensuring that business operations are efficient in terms of using as little resource as needed, and effective in terms of meeting customer requirements. It is concerned with managing the process that converts inputs (in the forms of materials, labour and energy) into outputs (in the form of goods and services.)

Operations traditionally refers to the production of goods and services separately, although the distinction between these two main types of operations is increasingly difficult to make as manufacturers tend to merge product and service offerings.

   a. AAAI
   c. A Stake in the Outcome
   b. Operations management
   d. A4e

24. _____ is a theory of management that analyzes and synthesizes workflows, with the objective of improving labour productivity. The core ideas of the theory were developed by Frederick Winslow Taylor in the 1880s and 1890s, and were first published in his monographs, Shop Management and The Principles of _____ Taylor believed that decisions based upon tradition and rules of thumb should be replaced by precise procedures developed after careful study of an individual at work.
   a. Value engineering
   c. Capacity planning
   b. Master production schedule
   d. Scientific management

25. _____, widely known as F. W. Taylor, was an American mechanical engineer who sought to improve industrial efficiency. He is regarded as the father of scientific management, and was one of the first management consultants.

Taylor was one of the intellectual leaders of the Efficiency Movement and his ideas, broadly conceived, were highly influential in the Progressive Era.

   a. Frederick Winslow Taylor
   c. Jonah Jacob Goldberg
   b. Douglas N. Daft
   d. Geoffrey Colvin

26. In economics, business, retail, and accounting, a _____ is the value of money that has been used up to produce something, and hence is not available for use anymore. In economics, a _____ is an alternative that is given up as a result of a decision. In business, the _____ may be one of acquisition, in which case the amount of money expended to acquire it is counted as _____.
   a. Cost overrun
   c. Cost allocation
   b. Cost
   d. Fixed costs

Chapter 1. Management and Its Evolution

27. _____ is the level of inventory that minimizes the total inventory holding costs and ordering costs. The framework used to determine this order quantity is also known as Wilson _____ Model. The model was developed by F. W. Harris in 1913.
   - a. Event management
   - b. Effective executive
   - c. Economic order quantity
   - d. Anti-leadership

28. _____ is a software based production planning and inventory control system used to manage manufacturing processes. Although it is not common nowadays, it is possible to conduct _____ by hand as well.

   An _____ system is intended to simultaneously meet three objectives:

   - Ensure materials and products are available for production and delivery to customers.
   - Maintain the lowest possible level of inventory.
   - Plan manufacturing activities, delivery schedules and purchasing activities.

   Manufacturing organizations, whatever their products, face the same daily practical problem - that customers want products to be available in a shorter time than it takes to make them. This means that some level of planning is required.
   - a. 33 Strategies of War
   - b. 28-hour day
   - c. 1990 Clean Air Act
   - d. Material requirements planning

29. _____ can be considered to have three main components: quality control, quality assurance and quality improvement. _____ is focused not only on product quality, but also the means to achieve it. _____ therefore uses quality assurance and control of processes as well as products to achieve more consistent quality.
   - a. 28-hour day
   - b. Total quality management
   - c. 1990 Clean Air Act
   - d. Quality management

30. _____ is one of the managerial functions like planning, organizing, staffing and directing. It is an important function because it helps to check the errors and to take the corrective action so that deviation from standards are minimized and stated goals of the organization are achieved in desired manner. According to modern concepts, _____ is a foreseeing action whereas earlier concept of _____ was used only when errors were detected. _____ in management means setting standards, measuring actual performance and taking corrective action.
   - a. Turnover
   - b. Schedule of reinforcement
   - c. Control
   - d. Decision tree pruning

31. In engineering and manufacturing, _____ and quality engineering are used in developing systems to ensure products or services are designed and produced to meet or exceed customer requirements. Refer to the definition by Merriam-Webster for further information. These systems are often developed in conjunction with other business and engineering disciplines using a cross-functional approach.
   - a. Single Minute Exchange of Die
   - b. Process capability
   - c. Statistical process control
   - d. Quality Control

32. _____ is a business management strategy aimed at embedding awareness of quality in all organizational processes. _____ has been widely used in manufacturing, education, hospitals, call centers, government, and service industries, as well as NASA space and science programs.

As defined by the International Organization for Standardization (ISO):

'_____ is a management approach for an organization, centered on quality, based on the participation of all its members and aiming at long-term success through customer satisfaction, and benefits to all members of the organization and to society.' ISO 8402:1994

One major aim is to reduce variation from every process so that greater consistency of effort is obtained. (Royse, D., Thyer, B., Padgett D., ' Logan T., 2006)

a. Quality management
b. 28-hour day
c. 1990 Clean Air Act
d. Total quality management

33. _____ according to Onuoha (2007) is the practice of starting new organizations or revitalizing mature organizations, particularly new businesses generally in response to identified opportunities. _____ is often a difficult undertaking, as a vast majority of new businesses fail. Entrepreneurial activities are substantially different depending on the type of organization that is being started.

a. AAAI
b. A Stake in the Outcome
c. Entrepreneurship
d. A4e

34. A _____ is a business that is privately owned and operated, with a small number of employees and relatively low volume of sales. The legal definition of 'small' often varies by country and industry, but is generally under 100 employees in the United States and under 50 employees in the European Union. In comparison, the definition of mid-sized business by the number of employees is generally under 500 in the U.S. and 250 for the European Union.

a. Critical Success Factor
b. Golden Boot Compensation
c. Pre-determined overhead rate
d. Small business

35. In a military context, the _____ is the line of authority and responsibility along which orders are passed within a military unit and between different units. The term is also used in a civilian management context describing comparable hierarchical structures of authority.

a. French leave
b. 28-hour day
c. 1990 Clean Air Act
d. Chain of command

36. The _____ is a form of reactivity whereby subjects improve an aspect of their behavior being experimentally measured simply in response to the fact that they are being studied, not in response to any particular experimental manipulation.

The term was coined in 1955 by Henry A. Landsberger when analyzing older experiments from 1924-1932 at the Hawthorne Works (outside Chicago.) Hawthorne Works had commissioned a study to see if its workers would become more productive in higher or lower levels of light.

a. Hawthorne effect
b. 1990 Clean Air Act
c. 28-hour day
d. 33 Strategies of War

Chapter 1. Management and Its Evolution

37. _____ Movement refers to those researchers of organizational development who study the behavior of people in groups, in particular workplace groups. It originated in the 1920s' Hawthorne studies, which examined the effects of social relations, motivation and employee satisfaction on factory productivity. The movement viewed workers in terms of their psychology and fit with companies, rather than as interchangeable parts.

   a. Work design
   b. Hersey-Blanchard situational theory
   c. Participatory management
   d. Human relations

38. Maslow's _____ is a theory in psychology, proposed by Abraham Maslow in his 1943 paper A Theory of Human Motivation, which he subsequently extended to include his observations of humans' innate curiosity.

Maslow's _____ is predetermined in order of importance. It is often depicted as a pyramid consisting of five levels: the lowest level is associated with physiological needs, while the uppermost level is associated with self-actualization needs, particularly those related to identity and purpose. Deficiency needs must be met first. Once these are met, seeking to satisfy growth needs drives personal growth. The higher needs in this hierarchy only come into focus when the lower needs in the pyramid are met.

   a. 33 Strategies of War
   b. 28-hour day
   c. Hierarchy of needs
   d. 1990 Clean Air Act

39. _____ and Theory Y are theories of human motivation created and developed by Douglas McGregor at the MIT Sloan School of Management in the 1960s that have been used in human resource management, organizational behavior, organizational communication and organizational development. They describe two very different attitudes toward workforce motivation. McGregor felt that companies followed either one or the other approach.

In _____, which many managers practice, management assumes employees are inherently lazy and will avoid work if they can. They inherently dislike work. Because of this, workers need to be closely supervised and comprehensive systems of controls developed.

   a. Management team
   b. Job enrichment
   c. Theory X
   d. Cash cow

40. Theory X and _____ are theories of human motivation created and developed by Douglas McGregor at the MIT Sloan School of Management in the 1960s that have been used in human resource management, organizational behavior, organizational communication and organizational development. They describe two very different attitudes toward workforce motivation. McGregor felt that companies followed either one or the other approach.

In _____, management assumes employees may be ambitious and self-motivated and exercise self-control. It is believed that employees enjoy their mental and physical work duties.

   a. Design leadership
   b. Business Workflow Analysis
   c. Theory Y
   d. Contingency theory

41. _____ is the principle that in open systems a given end state can be reached by many potential means. The term is due to Ludwig von Bertalanffy, the founder of General Systems Theory. He prefers this term, in contrast to 'goal', in describing complex systems' similar or convergent behavior.

a. AAAI
b. A4e
c. A Stake in the Outcome
d. Equifinality

42. _____ describes the situation when output from (or information about the result of) an event or phenomenon in the past will influence the same event/phenomenon in the present or future. When an event is part of a chain of cause-and-effect that forms a circuit or loop, then the event is said to 'feed back' into itself.

_____ is also a synonym for:

- _____ signal; the information about the initial event that is the basis for subsequent modification of the event.
- _____ loop; the causal path that leads from the initial generation of the _____ signal to the subsequent modification of the event.

_____ is a mechanism, process or signal that is looped back to control a system within itself. Such a loop is called a _____ loop.

a. 1990 Clean Air Act
b. Feedback loop
c. Positive feedback
d. Feedback

43. In management science, operations research and organizational development (OD), human organizations are viewed as systems (conceptual systems) of interacting components such as _____ or system aggregates, which are carriers of numerous complex processes and organizational structures. Organizational development theorist Peter Senge developed the notion of organizations as systems in his book The Fifth Discipline.

Systems thinking is a style of thinking/reasoning and problem solving.

a. 28-hour day
b. 1990 Clean Air Act
c. Systems thinking
d. Subsystems

44. _____ is the term used to describe a situation where different entities cooperate advantageously for a final outcome. Simply defined, it means that the whole is greater than the sum of the individual parts. Although the whole will be greater than each individual part, this is not the concept of _____.

a. 28-hour day
b. 1990 Clean Air Act
c. 33 Strategies of War
d. Synergy

45. _____ is the process by which the activities of an organisation, particularly those regarding decision-making, become concentrated within a particular location and/or group.

a. Corner office
b. Product innovation
c. Chief operating officer
d. Centralization

46. _____ is the process of dispersing decision-making governance closer to the people or citizen. It includes the dispersal of administration or governance in sectors or areas like engineering, management science, political science, political economy, sociology and economics. _____ is also possible in the dispersal of population and employment.

Chapter 1. Management and Its Evolution

a. Formula for Change
c. Frenemy
b. Decentralization
d. Business plan

47. _____ is a concept in ethics with several meanings. It is often used synonymously with such concepts as responsibility, answerability, enforcement, blameworthiness, liability and other terms associated with the expectation of account-giving. As an aspect of governance, it has been central to discussions related to problems in both the public and private (corporation) worlds.

a. A4e
c. A Stake in the Outcome
b. Usury
d. Accountability

48. An _____ is a practitioner of accountancy, which is the measurement, disclosure or provision of assurance about financial information that helps managers, investors, tax authorities and other decision makers make resource allocation decisions.

The word '_____' is derived from the French 'Compter' which took its origin from the Latin 'Computare'. The word was formerly written in English as 'Accomptant', but in process of time the word, which was always pronounced by dropping the 'p', became gradually changed both in pronunciation and in orthography to its present form.

a. A4e
c. Accountant
b. A Stake in the Outcome
d. AAAI

49. _____ for short is a descriptive term for certain executives in a business operation. It is also a formal title held by some business executives, most commonly in the hospitality industry.

A _____ has broad, overall responsibility for a business or organization. Whereas a manager may be responsible for one functional area, the _____ is responsible for all areas.

a. Chief knowledge officer
c. General manager
b. Chief technology officer
d. Managing director

50. _____ is an increasingly broadening term with which an organization, or other human system describes the combination of traditionally administrative personnel functions with acquisition and application of skills, knowledge and experience, Employee Relations and resource planning at various levels. The field draws upon concepts developed in Industrial/Organizational Psychology and System Theory. _____ has at least two related interpretations depending on context. The original usage derives from political economy and economics, where it was traditionally called labor, one of four factors of production although this perspective is changing as a function of new and ongoing research into more strategic approaches at national levels. This first usage is used more in terms of '_____ development', and can go beyond just organizations to the level of nations . The more traditional usage within corporations and businesses refers to the individuals within a firm or agency, and to the portion of the organization that deals with hiring, firing, training, and other personnel issues, typically referred to as `_____ management'.

a. Human resource management
c. Bradford Factor
b. Human resources
d. Progressive discipline

51. _____ is an integrated communications-based process through which individuals and communities discover that existing and newly-identified needs and wants may be satisfied by the products and services of others.

_____ is defined by the American _____ Association as the activity, set of institutions, and processes for creating, communicating, delivering, and exchanging offerings that have value for customers, clients, partners, and society at large. The term developed from the original meaning which referred literally to going to market, as in shopping, or going to a market to buy or sell goods or services.

a. Market development
c. Disruptive technology
b. Customer relationship management
d. Marketing

52. _____ or human capital flight is a large emigration of individuals with technical skills or knowledge, normally due to conflict, lack of opportunity, political instability, or health risks. _____ is usually regarded as an economic cost, since emigrants usually take with them the fraction of value of their training sponsored by the government. It is a parallel of capital flight which refers to the same movement of financial capital.

a. 33 Strategies of War
c. 28-hour day
b. 1990 Clean Air Act
d. Brain drain

53. The phrase _____, according to the Organization for Economic Co-operation and Development, refers to 'creative work undertaken on a systematic basis in order to increase the stock of knowledge, including knowledge of man, culture and society, and the use of this stock of knowledge to devise new applications [sic]'

New product design and development is more than often a crucial factor in the survival of a company. In an industry that is fast changing, firms must continually revise their design and range of products. This is necessary due to continuous technology change and development as well as other competitors and the changing preference of customers.

a. 1990 Clean Air Act
c. 33 Strategies of War
b. 28-hour day
d. Research and development

Chapter 2. Managing in a Global Environment

1. _____ is a term defined by the Oxford English Dictionary as an individual's 'course or progress through life '. It is usually considered to pertain to remunerative work (and sometimes also formal education.)

The etymology of the term is somewhat ironic in that it comes from the Latin word carrera, which means race .

a. Career planning
c. Spatial mismatch
b. Nursing shortage
d. Career

2. In organizational development (or OD), the study of _____ looks at:

- how individuals manage their careers within and between organizations
- and how organizations structure the career progress of their members, it can also be tied into succession planning within some organizations.

In personal development, _____ is:

- ' ... the total constellation of psychological, sociological, educational, physical, economic, and chance factors that combine to influence the nature and significance of work in the total lifespan of any given individual.'

- '... the lifelong psychological and behavioral processes as well as contextual influences shaping one's career over the life span. As such, _____ involves the person's creation of a career pattern, decision-making style, integration of life roles, values expression, and life-role self concepts.'

Figures in _____

- Jeff A. Brown
- Jesse B. Davis
- Caela Farren
- John L. Holland
- Kris Magnusson
- Frank Parsons
- Vance Peavy
- Edgar Schein
- Rino Schreuder
- Mark L. Savickas
- Donald Super

a. Sole proprietorship
c. Career development
b. Business process reengineering
d. Horizontal integration

3. _____ is the increase in the amount of the goods and services produced by an economy over time and is dependent on an increase in the creation of money. Growth is conventionally measured as the percent rate of increase in real gross domestic product, or real GDP. GDP is usually calculated in real terms, i.e. inflation-adjusted terms, in order to net out the effect of inflation on the price of the goods and services produced.

a. AAAI
b. Economic growth
c. A Stake in the Outcome
d. A4e

4. _____ is a form of applied ethics that examines ethical principles and moral or ethical problems that arise in a business environment. It applies to all aspects of business conduct and is relevant to the conduct of individuals and business organizations as a whole. Applied ethics is a field of ethics that deals with ethical questions in many fields such as medical, technical, legal and _____.

a. Corporate Sustainability
b. Facilitation payments
c. Hypernorms
d. Business ethics

5. The term '_____' refers to the concept of collecting information and attempting to spot a pattern in the information. In some fields of study, the term '_____' has more formally-defined meanings.

In project management _____ is a mathematical technique that uses historical results to predict future outcome.

a. Stepwise regression
b. Trend analysis
c. Regression analysis
d. Least squares

6. _____ or _____ data refers to selected population characteristics as used in government, marketing or opinion research, or the _____ profiles used in such research. Note the distinction from the term 'demography' Commonly-used _____s include race, age, income, disabilities, mobility (in terms of travel time to work or number of vehicles available), educational attainment, home ownership, employment status, and even location.

a. Abraham Harold Maslow
b. Adam Smith
c. Demographic
d. Affiliation

7. Procter is a surname, and may also refer to:

- Bryan Waller Procter (pseud. Barry Cornwall), English poet
- Goodwin Procter, American law firm
- _____, consumer products multinational

a. Downstream
b. Master and Servant Acts
c. Procter ' Gamble
d. Strict liability

8. A _____ is a general term that describes any government policy or regulation that restricts international trade. The barriers can take many forms, including the following terms that include many restrictions in international trade within multiple countries that import and export any items of trade.

- Import duty
- Import licenses
- Export licenses
- Import quotas
- Tariffs
- Subsidies
- Non-tariff barriers to trade
- Voluntary Export Restraints
- Local Content Requirements
- Embargo

Most _____s work on the same principle: the imposition of some sort of cost on trade that raises the price of the traded products. If two or more nations repeatedly use _____s against each other, then a trade war results.

a. Trade barrier
b. Customs brokerage
c. Trade creation
d. Most favoured nation

9. The _____ was the outcome of the failure of negotiating governments to create the International Trade Organization (ITO.) GATT was formed in 1947 and lasted until 1994, when it was replaced by the World Trade Organization. The Bretton Woods Conference had introduced the idea for an organization to regulate trade as part of a larger plan for economic recovery after World War II.

a. Multilateral treaty
b. General Agreement on Tariffs and Trade
c. 28-hour day
d. 1990 Clean Air Act

10. The _____ is an international organization designed by its founders to supervise and liberalize international trade. The organization officially commenced on 1 January 1995, under the Marrakesh Agreement, succeeding the 1947 General Agreement on Tariffs and Trade (GATT.)

The _____ deals with regulation of trade between participating countries; it provides a framework for negotiating and formalising trade agreements, and a dispute resolution process aimed at enforcing participants' adherence to _____ agreements which are signed by representatives of member governments and ratified by their parliaments.

a. 1990 Clean Air Act
b. Network planning and design
c. World Trade Organization
d. National Institute for Occupational Safety and Health

11. _____ is a type of trade policy that allows traders to act and transact without interference from government. Thus, the policy permits trading partners mutual gains from trade, with goods and services produced according to the theory of comparative advantage.

Under a _____ policy, prices are a reflection of true supply and demand, and are the sole determinant of resource allocation.

a. 33 Strategies of War
c. 1990 Clean Air Act
b. Free Trade
d. 28-hour day

12. _____ is a designated group of countries that have agreed to eliminate tariffs, quotas and preferences on most (if not all) goods and services traded between them. It can be considered the second stage of economic integration. Countries choose this kind of economic integration form if their economical structures are complementary.

a. Free trade area
c. 33 Strategies of War
b. 1990 Clean Air Act
d. 28-hour day

13. _____ is a broad label that refers to any individuals or households that use goods and services generated within the economy. The concept of a _____ is used in different contexts, so that the usage and significance of the term may vary.

Typically when business people and economists talk of _____s they are talking about person as _____, an aggregated commodity item with little individuality other than that expressed in the buy/not-buy decision.

a. 33 Strategies of War
c. 28-hour day
b. 1990 Clean Air Act
d. Consumer

14. _____ is an idea in the field of Organizational studies and management which describes the psychology, attitudes, experiences, beliefs and Values (personal and cultural values) of an organization. It has been defined as 'the specific collection of values and norms that are shared by people and groups in an organization and that control the way they interact with each other and with stakeholders outside the organization.'

This definition continues to explain organizational values also known as 'beliefs and ideas about what kinds of goals members of an organization should pursue and ideas about the appropriate kinds or standards of behavior organizational members should use to achieve these goals. From organizational values develop organizational norms, guidelines or expectations that prescribe appropriate kinds of behavior by employees in particular situations and control the behavior of organizational members towards one another.'

_____ is not the same as corporate culture.

a. Organizational development
c. Organizational effectiveness
b. Union shop
d. Organizational culture

15. _____ is an interdisciplinary field of science and the study of the nature of complex systems in nature, society, and science. More specifically, it is a framework by which one can analyze and/or describe any group of objects that work in concert to produce some result. This could be a single organism, any organization or society, or any electro-mechanical or informational artifact.

a. 1990 Clean Air Act
b. Systems thinking
c. 28-hour day
d. Systems theory

16. The 'business case for _____', theorizes that in a global marketplace, a company that employs a diverse workforce (both men and women, people of many generations, people from ethnically and racially diverse backgrounds etc.) is better able to understand the demographics of the marketplace it serves and is thus better equipped to thrive in that marketplace than a company that has a more limited range of employee demographics.

An additional corollary suggests that a company that supports the _____ of its workforce can also improve employee satisfaction, productivity and retention.

a. Diversity
b. Kanban
c. Virtual team
d. Trademark

17. An _____ is the negative aspects of human activity on the biophysical environment. Environmentalism, a social and environmental movement that started in the 1960s, focuses on addressing _____s through advocacy, education and activism.

Major current _____s are climate change, pollution and resource depletion.

a. Environmental issue
b. AAAI
c. A Stake in the Outcome
d. A4e

18. _____ in its literal sense is the process of transformation of local or regional phenomena into global ones. It can be described as a process by which the people of the world are unified into a single society and function together.

This process is a combination of economic, technological, sociocultural and political forces.

a. Histogram
b. Cost Management
c. Collaborative Planning, Forecasting and Replenishment
d. Globalization

19. _____ is subcontracting a process, such as product design or manufacturing, to a third-party company. The decision to outsource is often made in the interest of lowering cost or making better use of time and energy costs, redirecting or conserving energy directed at the competencies of a particular business, or to make more efficient use of land, labor, capital, (information) technology and resources. _____ became part of the business lexicon during the 1980s.

a. Opinion leadership
b. Outsourcing
c. Operant conditioning
d. Unemployment insurance

20. _____ is the strategic and coherent approach to the management of an organisation's most valued assets - the people working there who individually and collectively contribute to the achievement of the objectives of the business. The terms '_____' and 'human resources' (HR) have largely replaced the term 'personnel management' as a description of the processes involved in managing people in organizations. In simple sense, _____ means employing people, developing their resources, utilizing, maintaining and compensating their services in tune with the job and organizational requirement.

a. Revolving door syndrome
b. Job knowledge
c. Progressive discipline
d. Human resource management

21. In decision theory and estimation theory, the _____ of an estimator, $\hat{\theta}$, of an unknown parameter of the distribution, θ, is the expected value of the loss function

$$R(\theta, \hat{\theta}) = \mathbb{E}_\theta L(\theta, \hat{\theta}) = \int L(\theta, \hat{\theta}) \, dP_\theta.$$

where dP_θ is a probability measure parametrized by θ.

- For a scalar parameter θ and a quadratic loss function,

$$L(\theta, \hat{\theta}) = (\theta - \hat{\theta})^2$$

the _____ function becomes the mean squared error of the estimate,

$$R(\theta, \hat{\theta}) = E_\theta(\theta - \hat{\theta})^2$$

- In density estimation, the unknown parameter is probability density itself. The loss function is typically chosen to be a norm in an appropriate function space. For example, for L^2 norm,

$$L(f, \hat{f}) = \|f - \hat{f}\|_2^2$$

the _____ function becomes the mean integrated squared error

$$R(f, \hat{f}) = E\|f - \hat{f}\|^2$$

a. Financial modeling
b. Risk
c. Linear model
d. Risk aversion

22. _____ can be regarded as an outcome of mental processes (cognitive process) leading to the selection of a course of action among several alternatives. Every _____ process produces a final choice. The output can be an action or an opinion of choice.
a. 33 Strategies of War
b. 28-hour day
c. 1990 Clean Air Act
d. Decision making

Chapter 2. Managing in a Global Environment

23. _____ is a process of planning and controlling the performance or execution of any type of activity, such as:

- a project (project _____) or
- a process (process _____, sometimes referred to as the process performance measurement and management system.)

Organization's senior management is responsible for carrying out its _____.

a. Participatory management
b. Work design
c. Human Relations Movement
d. Management process

24. _____ is a reduction in the value of a currency with respect to other monetary units. In common modern usage, it specifically implies an official lowering of the value of a country's currency within a fixed exchange rate system, by which the monetary authority formally sets a new fixed rate with respect to a foreign reference currency. In contrast, depreciation is used for the unofficial decrease in the exchange rate in a floating exchange rate system.

a. 1990 Clean Air Act
b. 33 Strategies of War
c. 28-hour day
d. Devaluation

25. In finance, the _____s between two currencies specifies how much one currency is worth in terms of the other. It is the value of a foreign nation's currency in terms of the home nation's currency. For example an _____ of 102 Japanese yen to the United States dollar means that JPY 102 is worth the same as USD 1.

a. A Stake in the Outcome
b. AAAI
c. A4e
d. Exchange rate

26. The _____, signed in Paris, France, on March 20, 1883, was one of the first intellectual property treaties. As a result of this treaty, intellectual property systems, including patents, of any contracting state are accessible to the nationals of other states party to the Convention.

The 'Convention priority right', also called 'Paris Convention priority right' or 'Union priority right', was also established by this treaty.

a. Paris Convention for the Protection of Industrial Property
b. 1990 Clean Air Act
c. 28-hour day
d. 33 Strategies of War

27. _____ plant, and equipment, is a term used in accountancy for assets and property which cannot easily be converted into cash. This can be compared with current assets such as cash or bank accounts, which are described as liquid assets. In most cases, only tangible assets are referred to as fixed.

a. 28-hour day
b. 1990 Clean Air Act
c. Fixed asset
d. 33 Strategies of War

28. _____ consists of the mental process of thinking involved with the process of judging the merits of multiple options and selecting one of them for action. Some simple examples include deciding whether to get up in the morning or go back to sleep, or selecting a given route for a journey. More complex examples (often decisions that affect what a person thinks or their core beliefs) include choosing a lifestyle, religious affiliation, or political position.

Chapter 2. Managing in a Global Environment

a. Choice
b. Championship mobilization
c. Groups decision making
d. Trade study

29. A _____ is an entity formed between two or more parties to undertake economic activity together. The parties agree to create a new entity by both contributing equity, and they then share in the revenues, expenses, and control of the enterprise. The venture can be for one specific project only, or a continuing business relationship such as the Fuji Xerox _____.
a. Patent
b. Meritor Savings Bank v. Vinson
c. Civil Rights Act of 1991
d. Joint venture

30. An _____ is a person who has possession of an enterprise and assumes significant accountability for the inherent risks and the outcome. It is an ambitious leader who combines land, labor, and capital to create and market new goods or services. The term is a loanword from French and was first defined by the Irish economist Richard Cantillon.
a. Entrepreneur
b. A4e
c. A Stake in the Outcome
d. AAAI

31. _____ is the advantage gained by the initial occupant of a market segment. This advantage may stem from the fact that the first entrant can gain control of resources that followers may not be able to match. Sometimes the first mover is not able to capitalise on its advantage, leaving the opportunity for another firm to gain second-mover advantage.
a. Horizontal integration
b. Customer retention
c. First-mover advantage
d. Business ecosystem

32. In economics, business, retail, and accounting, a _____ is the value of money that has been used up to produce something, and hence is not available for use anymore. In economics, a _____ is an alternative that is given up as a result of a decision. In business, the _____ may be one of acquisition, in which case the amount of money expended to acquire it is counted as _____.
a. Cost overrun
b. Fixed costs
c. Cost
d. Cost allocation

33. _____ is exchange of capital, goods, and services across international borders or territories. In most countries, it represents a significant share of gross domestic product (GDP.) While _____ has been present throughout much of history , its economic, social, and political importance has been on the rise in recent centuries.
a. A4e
b. A Stake in the Outcome
c. AAAI
d. International trade

Chapter 2. Managing in a Global Environment

34. _____ refers to the movement of cash into or out of a business or financial product. It is usually measured during a specified, finite period of time. Measurement of _____ can be used

- to determine a project's rate of return or value. The time of _____s into and out of projects are used as inputs in financial models such as internal rate of return, and net present value.
- to determine problems with a business's liquidity. Being profitable does not necessarily mean being liquid. A company can fail because of a shortage of cash, even while profitable.
- as an alternate measure of a business's profits when it is believed that accrual accounting concepts do not represent economic realities. For example, a company may be notionally profitable but generating little operational cash (as may be the case for a company that barters its products rather than selling for cash.) In such a case, the company may be deriving additional operating cash by issuing shares evaluating default risk, re-investment requirements, etc.

_____ is a generic term used differently depending on the context. It may be defined by users for their own purposes.

a. Gross profit
b. Sweat equity
c. Cash flow
d. Gross profit margin

35. A _____ is a formal relationship between two or more parties to pursue a set of agreed upon goals or to meet a critical business need while remaining independent organizations.

Partners may provide the _____ with resources such as products, distribution channels, manufacturing capability, project funding, capital equipment, knowledge, expertise, or intellectual property. The alliance is a cooperation or collaboration which aims for a synergy where each partner hopes that the benefits from the alliance will be greater than those from individual efforts.

a. Process automation
b. Golden parachute
c. Strategic alliance
d. Farmshoring

36. A _____, in business matters, is an entity that is controlled by a bigger and more powerful entity. The controlled entity is called a company, corporation, or limited liability company and in some cases can be a government or state-owned enterprise, and the controlling entity is called its parent (or the parent company.) The reason for this distinction is that a lone company cannot be a _____ of any organization; only an entity representing a legal fiction as a separate entity can be a _____.

a. 33 Strategies of War
b. 28-hour day
c. 1990 Clean Air Act
d. Subsidiary

37. An _____ is a person temporarily or permanently residing in a country and culture other than that of the person's upbringing or legal residence. The word comes from the Latin ex and patria (country, fatherland.)

The term is sometimes used in the context of Westerners living in non-Western countries, although it is also used to describe Westerners living in other Western countries, such as Americans living in the United Kingdom, or Britons living in Spain.

Chapter 2. Managing in a Global Environment

a. A Stake in the Outcome
b. AAAI
c. A4e
d. Expatriate

38. A _____ is a name or trademark connected with a product or producer. _____s have become increasingly important components of culture and the economy, now being described as 'cultural accessories and personal philosophies'.

Some people distinguish the psychological aspect of a _____ from the experiential aspect.

a. Brand extension
b. Brand awareness
c. Brand loyalty
d. Brand

39. A _____ is a process in which a potential employee is evaluated by an employer for prospective employment in their company, organization and was established in the late 16th century.

A _____ typically precedes the hiring decision, and is used to evaluate the candidate. The interview is usually preceded by the evaluation of submitted résumés from interested candidates, then selecting a small number of candidates for interviews.

a. Split shift
b. Payrolling
c. Supported employment
d. Job interview

40. _____ is a mathematical science pertaining to the collection, analysis, interpretation or explanation, and presentation of data. It also provides tools for prediction and forecasting based on data. It is applicable to a wide variety of academic disciplines, from the natural and social sciences to the humanities, government and business.

a. Location parameter
b. Failure rate
c. Statistics
d. Simple moving average

41. A _____ is a person who alleges misconduct. More complex definitions may be used, but the issue is that the _____ usually faces reprisal. The misconduct may be classified in many ways; for example, a violation of a law, rule, regulation and/or a direct threat to public interest, such as fraud, health/safety violations, and corruption.

a. Whistleblower
b. 28-hour day
c. 1990 Clean Air Act
d. 33 Strategies of War

42. A _____ is typically described as a deliberate plan of action to guide decisions and achieve rational outcome(s). However, the term may also be used to denote what is actually done, even though it is unplanned.

The term may apply to government, private sector organizations and groups, and individuals.

a. 1990 Clean Air Act
b. 33 Strategies of War
c. 28-hour day
d. Policy

43. _____ is a concept in ethics with several meanings. It is often used synonymously with such concepts as responsibility, answerability, enforcement, blameworthiness, liability and other terms associated with the expectation of account-giving. As an aspect of governance, it has been central to discussions related to problems in both the public and private (corporation) worlds.

a. A Stake in the Outcome
b. Usury
c. A4e
d. Accountability

Chapter 3. Managing Social Responsibility and Ethics

1. _____ is a form of applied ethics that examines ethical principles and moral or ethical problems that arise in a business environment. It applies to all aspects of business conduct and is relevant to the conduct of individuals and business organizations as a whole. Applied ethics is a field of ethics that deals with ethical questions in many fields such as medical, technical, legal and _____.
   - a. Business ethics
   - b. Facilitation payments
   - c. Hypernorms
   - d. Corporate Sustainability

2. _____ can be regarded as an outcome of mental processes (cognitive process) leading to the selection of a course of action among several alternatives. Every _____ process produces a final choice. The output can be an action or an opinion of choice.
   - a. 28-hour day
   - b. Decision making
   - c. 33 Strategies of War
   - d. 1990 Clean Air Act

3. A _____ is typically described as a deliberate plan of action to guide decisions and achieve rational outcome(s.) However, the term may also be used to denote what is actually done, even though it is unplanned.

   The term may apply to government, private sector organizations and groups, and individuals.
   - a. 33 Strategies of War
   - b. 28-hour day
   - c. 1990 Clean Air Act
   - d. Policy

4. A _____ is a person who alleges misconduct. More complex definitions may be used, but the issue is that the _____ usually faces reprisal. The misconduct may be classified in many ways; for example, a violation of a law, rule, regulation and/or a direct threat to public interest, such as fraud, health/safety violations, and corruption.
   - a. Whistleblower
   - b. 1990 Clean Air Act
   - c. 33 Strategies of War
   - d. 28-hour day

5. _____ in its literal sense is the process of transformation of local or regional phenomena into global ones. It can be described as a process by which the people of the world are unified into a single society and function together.

   This process is a combination of economic, technological, sociocultural and political forces.
   - a. Globalization
   - b. Histogram
   - c. Collaborative Planning, Forecasting and Replenishment
   - d. Cost Management

6. The _____ of 2002 (Pub.L. 107-204, 116 Stat. 745, enacted July 30, 2002), also known as the Public Company Accounting Reform and Investor Protection Act of 2002 and commonly called Sarbanes-Oxley, Sarbox or SOX, is a United States federal law enacted on July 30, 2002, as a reaction to a number of major corporate and accounting scandals including those affecting Enron, Tyco International, Adelphia, Peregrine Systems and WorldCom.
   - a. Letter of credit
   - b. Sarbanes-Oxley Act of 2002
   - c. Fair Labor Standards Act
   - d. Sarbanes-Oxley Act

7. The _____, also known as the Public Company Accounting Reform and Investor Protection Act of 2002 and commonly called Sarbanes-Oxley, Sarbox or SOX, is a United States federal law enacted on July 30, 2002, as a reaction to a number of major corporate and accounting scandals including those affecting Enron, Tyco International, Adelphia, Peregrine Systems and WorldCom.

a. Letter of credit
b. Sarbanes-Oxley Act of 2002
c. Munn v. Illinois
d. MacPherson v. Buick Motor Co.

8. _____ is a method by which the job performance of an employee is evaluated _____ is a part of career development.

_____s are regular reviews of employee performance within organizations

Generally, the aims of a _____ are to:

- Give feedback on performance to employees.
- Identify employee training needs.
- Document criteria used to allocate organizational rewards.
- Form a basis for personnel decisions: salary increases, promotions, disciplinary actions, etc.
- Provide the opportunity for organizational diagnosis and development.
- Facilitate communication between employee and administraton
- Validate selection techniques and human resource policies to meet federal Equal Employment Opportunity requirements.

A common approach to assessing performance is to use a numerical or scalar rating system whereby managers are asked to score an individual against a number of objectives/attributes. In some companies, employees receive assessments from their manager, peers, subordinates and customers while also performing a self assessment.

a. Human resource management
b. Performance appraisal
c. Progressive discipline
d. Personnel management

9. _____ is a term defined by the Oxford English Dictionary as an individual's 'course or progress through life '. It is usually considered to pertain to remunerative work (and sometimes also formal education.)

The etymology of the term is somewhat ironic in that it comes from the Latin word carrera, which means race .

a. Career planning
b. Spatial mismatch
c. Career
d. Nursing shortage

10. In organizational development (or OD), the study of _____ looks at:

- how individuals manage their careers within and between organizations
- and how organizations structure the career progress of their members, it can also be tied into succession planning within some organizations.

Chapter 3. Managing Social Responsibility and Ethics

In personal development, _____ is:

- ' ... the total constellation of psychological, sociological, educational, physical, economic, and chance factors that combine to influence the nature and significance of work in the total lifespan of any given individual.'

- '... the lifelong psychological and behavioral processes as well as contextual influences shaping one's career over the life span. As such, _____ involves the person's creation of a career pattern, decision-making style, integration of life roles, values expression, and life-role self concepts.'

Figures in _____

- Jeff A. Brown
- Jesse B. Davis
- Caela Farren
- John L. Holland
- Kris Magnusson
- Frank Parsons
- Vance Peavy
- Edgar Schein
- Rino Schreuder
- Mark L. Savickas
- Donald Super

a. Horizontal integration
b. Sole proprietorship
c. Career development
d. Business process reengineering

11. The U.S. _____ is an independent agency of the United States government which holds primary responsibility for enforcing the federal securities laws and regulating the securities industry, the nation's stock and options exchanges, and other electronic securities markets. The SEC was created by section 4 of the Securities Exchange Act of 1934 (now codified as 15 U.S.C. § 78d and commonly referred to as the 1934 Act.)
   a. 1990 Clean Air Act
   b. 33 Strategies of War
   c. Securities and Exchange Commission
   d. 28-hour day

12. In economics, business, retail, and accounting, a _____ is the value of money that has been used up to produce something, and hence is not available for use anymore. In economics, a _____ is an alternative that is given up as a result of a decision. In business, the _____ may be one of acquisition, in which case the amount of money expended to acquire it is counted as _____.
   a. Fixed costs
   b. Cost allocation
   c. Cost
   d. Cost overrun

13. _____ is an advertisement in which a particular product specifically mentions a competitor by name for the express purpose of showing why the competitor is inferior to the product naming it.

This should not be confused with parody advertisements, where a fictional product is being advertised for the purpose of poking fun at the particular advertisement, nor should it be confused with the use of a coined brand name for the purpose of comparing the product without actually naming an actual competitor. ('Wikipedia tastes better and is less filling than the Encyclopedia Galactica.')

In the 1980s, during what has been referred to as the cola wars, soft-drink manufacturer Pepsi ran a series of advertisements where people, caught on hidden camera, in a blind taste test, chose Pepsi over rival Coca-Cola.

a. 1990 Clean Air Act
b. 28-hour day
c. 33 Strategies of War
d. Comparative advertising

14. The International Brotherhood of _____ is a labor union in the United States and Canada. Formed in 1903 by the merger of several local and regional locals of _____, the union now represents a diverse membership of blue-collar and professional workers in both the public and private sectors. The union had approximately 1.4 million members in 2007.

a. 1990 Clean Air Act
b. 28-hour day
c. 33 Strategies of War
d. Teamsters

15. A _____ is a relatively new executive level position at a corporation, company, organization typically reporting directly to the CEO or board of directors. The _____ is responsible for a brand's image, experience, and promise, and propagating it throughout all aspects of the company. The brand officer oversees marketing, advertising, design, public relations and customer service departments.

a. Chief brand officer
b. Director of communications
c. Purchasing manager
d. Chief executive officer

16. The _____ captures an expanded spectrum of values and criteria for measuring organizational success: economic, ecological and social. With the ratification of the United Nations and ICLEI _____ standard for urban and community accounting in early 2007, this became the dominant approach to public sector full cost accounting. Similar UN standards apply to natural capital and human capital measurement to assist in measurements required by _____, e.g. the ecoBudget standard for reporting ecological footprint.

a. Triple bottom line
b. 1990 Clean Air Act
c. 33 Strategies of War
d. 28-hour day

17. A _____ is one scenario provided for evaluation by respondents in a Choice Experiment. Responses are collected and used to create a Choice Model. Respondents are usually provided with a series of differing _____s for evaluation.

a. Choice Set
b. Computerized classification test
c. Pairwise comparison
d. Thurstone scale

18. _____ is one of the managerial functions like planning, organizing, staffing and directing. It is an important function because it helps to check the errors and to take the corrective action so that deviation from standards are minimized and stated goals of the organization are achieved in desired manner.According to modern concepts, _____ is a foreseeing action whereas earlier concept of _____ was used only when errors were detected. _____ in management means setting standards, measuring actual performance and taking corrective action.

a. Decision tree pruning
c. Schedule of reinforcement
b. Turnover
d. Control

19. Procter is a surname, and may also refer to:

- Bryan Waller Procter (pseud. Barry Cornwall), English poet
- Goodwin Procter, American law firm
- _____, consumer products multinational

a. Downstream
c. Strict liability
b. Procter ' Gamble
d. Master and Servant Acts

20. _____ is the point where a person stops employment completely. A person may also semi-retire and keep some sort of _____ job, out of choice rather than necessity. This usually happens upon reaching a determined age, when physical conditions don't allow the person to work any more (by illness or accident), or even for personal choice (usually in the presence of an adequate pension or personal savings.)
   a. Wrongful dismissal
   c. Termination of employment
   b. Severance package
   d. Retirement

21. The terms _____ or superannuation refer to a pension granted upon retirement . _____s may be set up by employers, insurance companies, the government or other institutions such as employer associations or trade unions. Called _____s in the USA, they are more commonly known as pension schemes in the UK and Ireland and superannuation plans in Australia.
   a. Salary calculator
   c. Real wage
   b. Wage
   d. Retirement plan

Chapter 4. Managing Organizational Culture and Change

1. _____ is an idea in the field of Organizational studies and management which describes the psychology, attitudes, experiences, beliefs and Values (personal and cultural values) of an organization. It has been defined as 'the specific collection of values and norms that are shared by people and groups in an organization and that control the way they interact with each other and with stakeholders outside the organization.'

This definition continues to explain organizational values also known as 'beliefs and ideas about what kinds of goals members of an organization should pursue and ideas about the appropriate kinds or standards of behavior organizational members should use to achieve these goals. From organizational values develop organizational norms, guidelines or expectations that prescribe appropriate kinds of behavior by employees in particular situations and control the behavior of organizational members towards one another.'

_____ is not the same as corporate culture.

- a. Union shop
- b. Organizational effectiveness
- c. Organizational development
- d. Organizational culture

2. The 'business case for _____', theorizes that in a global marketplace, a company that employs a diverse workforce (both men and women, people of many generations, people from ethnically and racially diverse backgrounds etc.) is better able to understand the demographics of the marketplace it serves and is thus better equipped to thrive in that marketplace than a company that has a more limited range of employee demographics.

An additional corollary suggests that a company that supports the _____ of its workforce can also improve employee satisfaction, productivity and retention.

- a. Virtual team
- b. Kanban
- c. Trademark
- d. Diversity

3. _____ can be regarded as an outcome of mental processes (cognitive process) leading to the selection of a course of action among several alternatives. Every _____ process produces a final choice. The output can be an action or an opinion of choice.
- a. 33 Strategies of War
- b. 1990 Clean Air Act
- c. 28-hour day
- d. Decision making

4. _____ has been described as the 'process of social influence in which one person can enlist the aid and support of others in the accomplishment of a common task' . A definition more inclusive of followers comes from Alan Keith of Genentech who said '_____ is ultimately about creating a way for people to contribute to making something extraordinary happen.'

_____ is one of the most salient aspects of the organizational context. However, defining _____ has been challenging.

- a. 1990 Clean Air Act
- b. 28-hour day
- c. Leadership
- d. Situational leadership

Chapter 4. Managing Organizational Culture and Change

5. _____ is one of the managerial functions like planning, organizing, staffing and directing. It is an important function because it helps to check the errors and to take the corrective action so that deviation from standards are minimized and stated goals of the organization are achieved in desired manner. According to modern concepts, _____ is a foreseeing action whereas earlier concept of _____ was used only when errors were detected. _____ in management means setting standards, measuring actual performance and taking corrective action.

   a. Decision tree pruning
   b. Schedule of reinforcement
   c. Turnover
   d. Control

6. The _____ in statistical process control is a tool used to determine whether a manufacturing or business process is in a state of statistical control or not.

If the chart indicates that the process is currently under control then it can be used with confidence to predict the future performance of the process. If the chart indicates that the process being monitored is not in control, the pattern it reveals can help determine the source of variation to be eliminated to bring the process back into control.

   a. Time series analysis
   b. Failure rate
   c. Control chart
   d. Simple moving average

7. An _____ is the negative aspects of human activity on the biophysical environment. Environmentalism, a social and environmental movement that started in the 1960s, focuses on addressing _____s through advocacy, education and activism.

Major current _____s are climate change, pollution and resource depletion.

   a. AAAI
   b. A Stake in the Outcome
   c. A4e
   d. Environmental issue

8. _____ is unwelcome harassment of a sexual nature, or based upon the receiving party's sex or gender. In some contexts or circumstances, _____ may be illegal. It includes a range of behavior from seemingly mild transgressions and annoyances to actual sexual abuse or sexual assault.

   a. 1990 Clean Air Act
   b. Hypernorms
   c. 28-hour day
   d. Sexual harassment

9. _____ is a business management strategy aimed at embedding awareness of quality in all organizational processes. _____ has been widely used in manufacturing, education, hospitals, call centers, government, and service industries, as well as NASA space and science programs.

As defined by the International Organization for Standardization (ISO):

   '_____ is a management approach for an organization, centered on quality, based on the participation of all its members and aiming at long-term success through customer satisfaction, and benefits to all members of the organization and to society.' ISO 8402:1994

One major aim is to reduce variation from every process so that greater consistency of effort is obtained. (Royse, D., Thyer, B., Padgett D., ' Logan T., 2006)

a. 1990 Clean Air Act
c. 28-hour day
b. Quality management
d. Total quality management

10. _____ can be considered to have three main components: quality control, quality assurance and quality improvement. _____ is focused not only on product quality, but also the means to achieve it. _____ therefore uses quality assurance and control of processes as well as products to achieve more consistent quality.

a. 28-hour day
c. Total quality management
b. 1990 Clean Air Act
d. Quality management

11. The _____ (Situation, Task, Action, Result) format is a job interview technique used by interviewers to gather all the relevant information about a specific capability that the job requires. This interview format is said to have a higher degree of predictability of future on-the-job performance than the traditional interview.

- Situation: The interviewer wants you to present a recent challenge and situation in which you found yourself.
- Task: What did you have to achieve? The interviewer will be looking to see what you were trying to achieve from the situation.
- Action: What did you do? The interviewer will be looking for information on what you did, why you did it and what were the alternatives.
- Results: What was the outcome of your actions? What did you achieve through your actions and did you meet your objectives. What did you learn from this experience and have you used this learning since?

a. Phrase completion
c. Rasch models
b. Competency-based job descriptions
d. Star

12. _____ of the learning curve effect and the closely related experience curve effect express the relationship between equations for experience and efficiency or between efficiency gains and investment in the effort. The experience of 'learning curves' was first observed by the 19th Century German psychologist Hermann Ebbinghaus according to the difficulty of memorizing varying numbers of verbal stimuli, and subsequent learning about the complex processes of learning are discussed in the

The rule used for representing the learning curve effect states that the more times a task has been performed, the less time will be required on each subsequent iteration.

a. Point biserial correlation coefficient
c. Models
b. Distribution
d. Spatial Decision Support Systems

13. _____ is a subfield of the larger discipline of communication studies. _____, as a field, is the consideration, analysis, and criticism of the role of communication in organizational contexts.

The field traces its lineage through business information, business communication, and early mass communication studies published in the 1930s through the 1950s.

a. A Stake in the Outcome
b. A4e
c. Organizational communication
d. AAAI

14. _____ is a form of applied ethics that examines ethical principles and moral or ethical problems that arise in a business environment. It applies to all aspects of business conduct and is relevant to the conduct of individuals and business organizations as a whole. Applied ethics is a field of ethics that deals with ethical questions in many fields such as medical, technical, legal and _____.

a. Facilitation payments
b. Corporate Sustainability
c. Hypernorms
d. Business ethics

15. _____ is a company-wide computer software system used to manage and coordinate all the resources, information, and functions of a business from shared data stores.

An _____ system has a service-oriented architecture with modular hardware and software units and 'services' that communicate on a local area network. The modular design allows a business to add or reconfigure modules (perhaps from different vendors) while preserving data integrity in one shared database that may be centralized or distributed.

a. A4e
b. AAAI
c. A Stake in the Outcome
d. Enterprise resource planning

Chapter 5. Managing the Planning Process

1. _____ is used to assign the available resources in an economic way. It is part of resource management.

In strategic planning,is a plan for using available resources, for example human resources, especially in the near term, to achieve goals for the future.

- a. Resource allocation
- b. 33 Strategies of War
- c. 28-hour day
- d. 1990 Clean Air Act

2. _____ is something that a firm can do well and that meets the following three conditions:

Competencies are things that companys execute well across several business units or product sectors.

Firms usually have few competencies, but these are usually less liable to change rapidly.

1. It provides consumer benefits
2. It is not easy for competitors to imitate
3. It can be leveraged widely to many products and markets.

A _____ can take various forms, including technical/subject matter know-how, a reliable process and/or close relationships with customers and suppliers (Mascarenhas et al. 1998.)

- a. Learning-by-doing
- b. Dominant Design
- c. NAIRU
- d. Core competency

3. _____ was first described by Barry M. Staw in his 1976 paper, 'Knee deep in the big muddy: A study of escalating commitment to a chosen course of action'. More recently the term Sunk cost fallacy has been used to describe the phenomenon where people justify increased investment in a decision, based on the cumulative prior investment, despite new evidence suggesting that the decision was probably wrong. Such investment may include money , time, or -- in the case of military strategy -- human lives.

- a. A Stake in the Outcome
- b. Open Options
- c. A4e
- d. Escalation of commitment

4. _____ is a strategic planning method that some organizations use to make flexible long-term plans. It is in large part an adaptation and generalization of classic methods used by military intelligence.

The original method was that a group of analysts would generate simulation games for policy makers. In business applications, the emphasis on gaming the behavior of opponents was reduced (shifting more toward a game against nature). At Royal Dutch/Shell for example, _____ was viewed as changing mindsets about the exogenous part of the world, prior to formulating specific strategies.

- a. Labour productivity
- b. Time and attendance
- c. Retroactive overtime
- d. Scenario planning

Chapter 5. Managing the Planning Process

5. Procter is a surname, and may also refer to:

- Bryan Waller Procter (pseud. Barry Cornwall), English poet
- Goodwin Procter, American law firm
- _____, consumer products multinational

a. Master and Servant Acts
b. Procter ' Gamble
c. Strict liability
d. Downstream

6. An _____ is the negative aspects of human activity on the biophysical environment. Environmentalism, a social and environmental movement that started in the 1960s, focuses on addressing _____s through advocacy, education and activism.

Major current _____s are climate change, pollution and resource depletion.

a. AAAI
b. A4e
c. A Stake in the Outcome
d. Environmental issue

7. _____ is an advertisement in which a particular product specifically mentions a competitor by name for the express purpose of showing why the competitor is inferior to the product naming it.

This should not be confused with parody advertisements, where a fictional product is being advertised for the purpose of poking fun at the particular advertisement, nor should it be confused with the use of a coined brand name for the purpose of comparing the product without actually naming an actual competitor. ('Wikipedia tastes better and is less filling than the Encyclopedia Galactica.')

In the 1980s, during what has been referred to as the cola wars, soft-drink manufacturer Pepsi ran a series of advertisements where people, caught on hidden camera, in a blind taste test, chose Pepsi over rival Coca-Cola.

a. 33 Strategies of War
b. 28-hour day
c. Comparative advertising
d. 1990 Clean Air Act

8. _____ is a process of agreeing upon objectives within an organization so that management and employees agree to the objectives and understand what they are in the organization.

The term '_____' was first popularized by Peter Drucker in his 1954 book 'The Practice of Management'.

The essence of _____ is participative goal setting, choosing course of actions and decision making.

a. Clean sheet review
b. Job enrichment
c. Business economics
d. Management by objectives

9. _____ is the term used to describe a situation where different entities cooperate advantageously for a final outcome. Simply defined, it means that the whole is greater than the sum of the individual parts. Although the whole will be greater than each individual part, this is not the concept of _____.

Chapter 5. Managing the Planning Process

a. 28-hour day
b. 1990 Clean Air Act
c. 33 Strategies of War
d. Synergy

10. _____ is one of the managerial functions like planning, organizing, staffing and directing. It is an important function because it helps to check the errors and to take the corrective action so that deviation from standards are minimized and stated goals of the organization are achieved in desired manner. According to modern concepts, _____ is a foreseeing action whereas earlier concept of _____ was used only when errors were detected. _____ in management means setting standards, measuring actual performance and taking corrective action.

a. Schedule of reinforcement
b. Turnover
c. Decision tree pruning
d. Control

11. _____ refers to the movement of cash into or out of a business or financial product. It is usually measured during a specified, finite period of time. Measurement of _____ can be used

- to determine a project's rate of return or value. The time of _____s into and out of projects are used as inputs in financial models such as internal rate of return, and net present value.
- to determine problems with a business's liquidity. Being profitable does not necessarily mean being liquid. A company can fail because of a shortage of cash, even while profitable.
- as an alternate measure of a business's profits when it is believed that accrual accounting concepts do not represent economic realities. For example, a company may be notionally profitable but generating little operational cash (as may be the case for a company that barters its products rather than selling for cash.) In such a case, the company may be deriving additional operating cash by issuing shares evaluating default risk, re-investment requirements, etc.

_____ is a generic term used differently depending on the context. It may be defined by users for their own purposes.

a. Gross profit
b. Sweat equity
c. Gross profit margin
d. Cash flow

12. _____ is the discipline of planning, organizing and managing resources to bring about the successful completion of specific project goals and objectives. It is often closely related to and sometimes conflated with Program management.

A project is a finite endeavor--having specific start and completion dates--undertaken to meet particular goals and objectives, usually to bring about beneficial change or added value.

a. Project engineer
b. Work package
c. Precedence diagram
d. Project management

13. A _____ is a set of instructions having the force of a directive, covering those features of operations that lend themselves to a definite or standardized procedure without loss of effectiveness. Standard Operating Policies and Procedures can be effective catalysts to drive performance improvement and improving organizational results.

a. Standard operating procedure
b. Risk-benefit analysis
c. Longitudinal study
d. 1990 Clean Air Act

Chapter 5. Managing the Planning Process 35

14. _____ is a form of social influence. It is the process of guiding people and oneself toward the adoption of an idea, attitude, or action by rational and symbolic (though not always logical) means. It is strategy of problem-solving relying on 'appeals' rather than coercion.

a. Self-enhancement
b. Social loafing
c. Personal space
d. Persuasion

15. _____ describes the situation when output from (or information about the result of) an event or phenomenon in the past will influence the same event/phenomenon in the present or future. When an event is part of a chain of cause-and-effect that forms a circuit or loop, then the event is said to 'feed back' into itself.

_____ is also a synonym for:

- _____ signal; the information about the initial event that is the basis for subsequent modification of the event.
- _____ loop; the causal path that leads from the initial generation of the _____ signal to the subsequent modification of the event.

_____ is a mechanism, process or signal that is looped back to control a system within itself. Such a loop is called a _____ loop.

a. 1990 Clean Air Act
b. Positive feedback
c. Feedback loop
d. Feedback

16. A _____ is a name or trademark connected with a product or producer. _____s have become increasingly important components of culture and the economy, now being described as 'cultural accessories and personal philosophies'.

Some people distinguish the psychological aspect of a _____ from the experiential aspect.

a. Brand extension
b. Brand loyalty
c. Brand
d. Brand awareness

Chapter 6. Decision Making

1. _____ can be regarded as an outcome of mental processes (cognitive process) leading to the selection of a course of action among several alternatives. Every _____ process produces a final choice. The output can be an action or an opinion of choice.

   a. 33 Strategies of War
   b. 28-hour day
   c. 1990 Clean Air Act
   d. Decision making

2. _____ refers to a range of skills, tools, and techniques used to manage time when accomplishing specific tasks, projects and goals. This set encompass a wide scope of activities, and these include planning, allocating, setting goals, delegation, analysis of time spent, monitoring, organizing, scheduling, and prioritizing. Initially _____ referred to just business or work activities, but eventually the term broadened to include personal activities also.

   a. Cash cow
   b. Formula for Change
   c. Voice of the customer
   d. Time management

3. In decision theory and estimation theory, the _____ of an estimator, $\hat{\theta}$, of an unknown parameter of the distribution, θ, is the expected value of the loss function

$$R(\theta, \hat{\theta}) = \mathbb{E}_\theta L(\theta, \hat{\theta}) = \int L(\theta, \hat{\theta})\, dP_\theta.$$

where dP_θ is a probability measure parametrized by θ.

- For a scalar parameter θ and a quadratic loss function,

$$L(\theta, \hat{\theta}) = (\theta - \hat{\theta})^2$$

  the _____ function becomes the mean squared error of the estimate,

$$R(\theta, \hat{\theta}) = E_\theta (\theta - \hat{\theta})^2$$

- In density estimation, the unknown parameter is probability density itself. The loss function is typically chosen to be a norm in an appropriate function space. For example, for L^2 norm,

$$L(f, \hat{f}) = \|f - \hat{f}\|_2^2$$

  the _____ function becomes the mean integrated squared error

$$R(f, \hat{f}) = E\|f - \hat{f}\|^2$$

   a. Risk aversion
   b. Financial modeling
   c. Linear model
   d. Risk

Chapter 6. Decision Making

4. _____ is an advertisement in which a particular product specifically mentions a competitor by name for the express purpose of showing why the competitor is inferior to the product naming it.

This should not be confused with parody advertisements, where a fictional product is being advertised for the purpose of poking fun at the particular advertisement, nor should it be confused with the use of a coined brand name for the purpose of comparing the product without actually naming an actual competitor. ('Wikipedia tastes better and is less filling than the Encyclopedia Galactica.')

In the 1980s, during what has been referred to as the cola wars, soft-drink manufacturer Pepsi ran a series of advertisements where people, caught on hidden camera, in a blind taste test, chose Pepsi over rival Coca-Cola.

a. 1990 Clean Air Act
b. 33 Strategies of War
c. Comparative advertising
d. 28-hour day

5. A _____ is a relatively new executive level position at a corporation, company, organization typically reporting directly to the CEO or board of directors. The _____ is responsible for a brand's image, experience, and promise, and propagating it throughout all aspects of the company. The brand officer oversees marketing, advertising, design, public relations and customer service departments.

a. Chief brand officer
b. Purchasing manager
c. Chief executive officer
d. Director of communications

6. A _____ is an alliance among individuals or groups, during which they cooperate in joint action, each in his own self-interest, joining forces together for a common cause. This alliance may be temporary or a matter of convenience. A _____ thus differs from a more formal covenant.

a. Coalition
b. 33 Strategies of War
c. 1990 Clean Air Act
d. 28-hour day

7. _____ is one of the managerial functions like planning, organizing, staffing and directing. It is an important function because it helps to check the errors and to take the corrective action so that deviation from standards are minimized and stated goals of the organization are achieved in desired manner. According to modern concepts, _____ is a foreseeing action whereas earlier concept of _____ was used only when errors were detected. _____ in management means setting standards, measuring actual performance and taking corrective action.

a. Decision tree pruning
b. Schedule of reinforcement
c. Turnover
d. Control

8. The _____ is a performance management tool for measuring whether the smaller-scale operational activities of a company are aligned with its larger-scale objectives in terms of vision and strategy.

By focusing not only on financial outcomes but also on the operational, marketing and developmental inputs to these, the _____ helps provide a more comprehensive view of a business, which in turn helps organizations act in their best long-term interests. This tool is also being used to address business response to climate change and greenhouse gas emissions.

a. Management development
b. Middle management
c. Commercial management
d. Balanced scorecard

Chapter 6. Decision Making

9. _____ was first described by Barry M. Staw in his 1976 paper, 'Knee deep in the big muddy: A study of escalating commitment to a chosen course of action'. More recently the term Sunk cost fallacy has been used to describe the phenomenon where people justify increased investment in a decision, based on the cumulative prior investment, despite new evidence suggesting that the decision was probably wrong. Such investment may include money, time, or -- in the case of military strategy -- human lives.

   a. A Stake in the Outcome
   b. A4e
   c. Open Options
   d. Escalation of commitment

10. _____ of the learning curve effect and the closely related experience curve effect express the relationship between equations for experience and efficiency or between efficiency gains and investment in the effort. The experience of 'learning curves' was first observed by the 19th Century German psychologist Hermann Ebbinghaus according to the difficulty of memorizing varying numbers of verbal stimuli, and subsequent learning about the complex processes of learning are discussed in the

The rule used for representing the learning curve effect states that the more times a task has been performed, the less time will be required on each subsequent iteration.

   a. Models
   b. Point biserial correlation coefficient
   c. Distribution
   d. Spatial Decision Support Systems

11. _____ is a concept based on the fact that rationality of individuals is limited by the information they have, the cognitive limitations of their minds, and the finite amount of time they have to make decisions. This contrasts with the concept of rationality as optimization. Another way to look at _____ is that, because decision-makers lack the ability and resources to arrive at the optimal solution, they instead apply their rationality only after having greatly simplified the choices available.

   a. Mixed strategy
   b. Transferable utility
   c. Bounded rationality
   d. Complete information

12. _____ is an adjective for experience-based techniques that help in problem solving, learning and discovery. A _____ method is particularly used to rapidly come to a solution that is hoped to be close to the best possible answer, or 'optimal solution'. _____s are 'rules of thumb', educated guesses, intuitive judgments or simply common sense.

   a. 1990 Clean Air Act
   b. Heuristic
   c. 28-hour day
   d. Representativeness

13. _____ is decision making in groups consisting of multiple members/entities. The challenge of group decision is deciding what action a group should take. There are various systems designed to solve this problem.

   a. Groups decision making
   b. Control of Substances Hazardous to Health Regulations 2002
   c. Collaborative Planning, Forecasting and Replenishment
   d. Genbutsu

Chapter 6. Decision Making

14. _____ is a type of thought exhibited by group members who try to minimize conflict and reach consensus without critically testing, analyzing, and evaluating ideas. Individual creativity, uniqueness, and independent thinking are lost in the pursuit of group cohesiveness, as are the advantages of reasonable balance in choice and thought that might normally be obtained by making decisions as a group. During _____, members of the group avoid promoting viewpoints outside the comfort zone of consensus thinking.

 a. Groupthink
 b. Psychological statistics
 c. Self-report inventory
 d. Diffusion of responsibility

15. _____ has been described as the 'process of social influence in which one person can enlist the aid and support of others in the accomplishment of a common task'. A definition more inclusive of followers comes from Alan Keith of Genentech who said '_____ is ultimately about creating a way for people to contribute to making something extraordinary happen.'

_____ is one of the most salient aspects of the organizational context. However, defining _____ has been challenging.

 a. Situational leadership
 b. 28-hour day
 c. 1990 Clean Air Act
 d. Leadership

16. _____ is a group creativity technique designed to generate a large number of ideas for the solution of a problem. The method was first popularized in the late 1930s by Alex Faickney Osborn in a book called Applied Imagination. Osborn proposed that groups could double their creative output with _____.

 a. Affiliation
 b. Abraham Harold Maslow
 c. Adam Smith
 d. Brainstorming

17. The _____ is a decision making method for use among groups of many sizes, who want to make their decision quickly, as by a vote, but want everyone's opinions taken into account (as opposed to traditional voting, where only the largest group is considered). The method of tallying is the difference. First, every member of the group gives their view of the solution, with a short explanation.

 a. Decision model
 b. Hierarchical Decision Process
 c. Belief decision matrix
 d. Nominal group technique

18. The _____ is a systematic, interactive forecasting method which relies on a panel of independent experts. The carefully selected experts answer questionnaires in two or more rounds. After each round, a facilitator provides an anonymous summary of the experts' forecasts from the previous round as well as the reasons they provided for their judgments.

 a. Hoshin Kanri
 b. Quality function deployment
 c. Delphi method
 d. Learning organization

19. A _____ is a name or trademark connected with a product or producer. _____s have become increasingly important components of culture and the economy, now being described as 'cultural accessories and personal philosophies'.

Some people distinguish the psychological aspect of a _____ from the experiential aspect.

a. Brand
b. Brand extension
c. Brand awareness
d. Brand loyalty

20. _____ is a concept in ethics with several meanings. It is often used synonymously with such concepts as responsibility, answerability, enforcement, blameworthiness, liability and other terms associated with the expectation of account-giving. As an aspect of governance, it has been central to discussions related to problems in both the public and private (corporation) worlds.

a. Usury
b. A4e
c. A Stake in the Outcome
d. Accountability

Chapter 7. Strategic Management

1. _____ is, in very basic words, a position a firm occupies against its competitors.

According to Michael Porter, the three methods for creating a sustainable _____ are through:

1. Cost leadership

2. Differentiation

3. Focus (economics)

   a. 28-hour day   b. Competitive advantage
   c. Theory Z   d. 1990 Clean Air Act

2. In game theory, an _____ is a set of moves or strategies taken by the players, or their payoffs resulting from the actions or strategies taken by all players. The two are complementary in that given knowledge of the set of strategies of all players, the final state of the game is known, as are any relevant payoffs. In a game where chance or a random event is involved, the _____ is not known from only the set of strategies, but is only realized when the random event(s) are realized.
   a. A4e   b. A Stake in the Outcome
   c. AAAI   d. Outcome

3. _____ is a strategic planning method used to evaluate the Strengths, Weaknesses, Opportunities, and Threats involved in a project or in a business venture. It involves specifying the objective of the business venture or project and identifying the internal and external factors that are favorable and unfavorable to achieving that objective. The technique is credited to Albert Humphrey, who led a convention at Stanford University in the 1960s and 1970s using data from Fortune 500 companies.
   a. Market share   b. SWOT analysis
   c. Marketing   d. Corporate image

4. _____ in marketing and strategic management is an assessment of the strengths and weaknesses of current and potential competitors. This analysis provides both an offensive and defensive strategic context through which to identify opportunities and threats. Competitor profiling coalesces all of the relevant sources of _____ into one framework in the support of efficient and effective strategy formulation, implementation, monitoring and adjustment.
   a. Competitor or Competitive Intelligence   b. 1990 Clean Air Act
   c. 28-hour day   d. Competitor analysis

5. In probability theory, a probability distribution is called _____ if its cumulative distribution function is _____. This is equivalent to saying that for random variables X with the distribution in question, $Pr[X = a] = 0$ for all real numbers a, i.e.: the probability that X attains the value a is zero, for any number a. If the distribution of X is _____ then X is called a _____ random variable.
   a. Connectionist expert systems   b. Decision tree pruning
   c. Pay Band   d. Continuous

6. _____ is the production of large amounts of standardized products, including and especially on assembly lines. The concepts of _____ are applied to various kinds of products, from fluids and particulates handled in bulk to discrete solid parts to assemblies of such parts

_____ of assemblies typically uses electric-motor-powered moving tracks or conveyor belts to move partially complete products to workers, who perform simple repetitive tasks.

a. 1990 Clean Air Act
c. 33 Strategies of War
b. 28-hour day
d. Mass production

7. _____ is an advertisement in which a particular product specifically mentions a competitor by name for the express purpose of showing why the competitor is inferior to the product naming it.

This should not be confused with parody advertisements, where a fictional product is being advertised for the purpose of poking fun at the particular advertisement, nor should it be confused with the use of a coined brand name for the purpose of comparing the product without actually naming an actual competitor. ('Wikipedia tastes better and is less filling than the Encyclopedia Galactica.')

In the 1980s, during what has been referred to as the cola wars, soft-drink manufacturer Pepsi ran a series of advertisements where people, caught on hidden camera, in a blind taste test, chose Pepsi over rival Coca-Cola.

a. 1990 Clean Air Act
c. 28-hour day
b. 33 Strategies of War
d. Comparative advertising

8. _____ is the process of estimation in unknown situations. Prediction is a similar, but more general term. Both can refer to estimation of time series, cross-sectional or longitudinal data.

a. Forecasting
c. 1990 Clean Air Act
b. 28-hour day
d. 33 Strategies of War

9. _____ or _____ data refers to selected population characteristics as used in government, marketing or opinion research, or the _____ profiles used in such research. Note the distinction from the term 'demography' Commonly-used _____s include race, age, income, disabilities, mobility (in terms of travel time to work or number of vehicles available), educational attainment, home ownership, employment status, and even location.

a. Affiliation
c. Adam Smith
b. Abraham Harold Maslow
d. Demographic

10. The term '_____' refers to the concept of collecting information and attempting to spot a pattern in the information. In some fields of study, the term '_____' has more formally-defined meanings.

In project management _____ is a mathematical technique that uses historical results to predict future outcome.

a. Least squares
c. Regression analysis
b. Stepwise regression
d. Trend analysis

11. A _____ is a name or trademark connected with a product or producer. _____s have become increasingly important components of culture and the economy, now being described as 'cultural accessories and personal philosophies'.

Some people distinguish the psychological aspect of a _____ from the experiential aspect.

a. Brand
b. Brand loyalty
c. Brand extension
d. Brand awareness

12. The _____ requires the Federal government to investigate and pursue trusts, companies and organizations suspected of violating the Act. It was the first United States Federal statute to limit cartels and monopolies, and today still forms the basis for most antitrust litigation by the federal government.

a. Sherman Antitrust Act
b. 1990 Clean Air Act
c. 33 Strategies of War
d. 28-hour day

13. The International Brotherhood of _____ is a labor union in the United States and Canada. Formed in 1903 by the merger of several local and regional locals of _____, the union now represents a diverse membership of blue-collar and professional workers in both the public and private sectors. The union had approximately 1.4 million members in 2007.

a. 28-hour day
b. 1990 Clean Air Act
c. Teamsters
d. 33 Strategies of War

14. An _____ is the negative aspects of human activity on the biophysical environment. Environmentalism, a social and environmental movement that started in the 1960s, focuses on addressing _____s through advocacy, education and activism.

Major current _____s are climate change, pollution and resource depletion.

a. A Stake in the Outcome
b. A4e
c. AAAI
d. Environmental issue

15. _____ in its literal sense is the process of transformation of local or regional phenomena into global ones. It can be described as a process by which the people of the world are unified into a single society and function together.

This process is a combination of economic, technological, sociocultural and political forces.

a. Histogram
b. Cost Management
c. Collaborative Planning, Forecasting and Replenishment
d. Globalization

16. In economics and especially in the theory of competition, _____ are obstacles in the path of a firm that make it difficult to enter a given market.

_____ are the source of a firm's pricing power - the ability of a firm to raise prices without losing all its customers.

The term refers to hindrances that an individual may face while trying to gain entrance into a profession or trade.

a. Predatory pricing
b. Barriers to entry
c. 28-hour day
d. 1990 Clean Air Act

17. _____ is the self-government of a nation, country or some portion thereof, generally exercising sovereignty.

The term _____ is used in contrast to subjugation, which refers to a region as a 'territory' --subject to the political and military control of an external government. The word is sometimes used in a weaker sense to contrast with hegemony, the indirect control of one nation by another, more powerful nation.

a. AAAI
b. Independence
c. A4e
d. A Stake in the Outcome

18. The _____ is an economic tool used to determine the strategic resources available to a firm. The fundamental principle of the _____ is that the basis for a competitive advantage of a firm lies primarily in the application of the bundle of valuable resources at the firm's disposal (Wernerfelt, 1984, p172; Rumelt, 1984, p557-558.) To transform a short-run competitive advantage into a sustained competitive advantage requires that these resources are heterogeneous in nature and not perfectly mobile (Barney, 1991, p105-106; Peteraf, 1993, p180).

a. Business philosophy
b. Frenemy
c. Resource-based view
d. Catfish effect

19. A _____ is a concept used in strategic management that groups companies within an industry that have similar business models or similar combinations of strategies. For example, the restaurant industry can be divided into several _____s including fast-food and fine-dining based on variables such as preparation time, pricing, and presentation. The number of groups within an industry and their composition depends on the dimensions used to define the groups.

a. Strategic group
b. Corporate strategy
c. Strategic business unit
d. Strategic drift

20. _____ is something that a firm can do well and that meets the following three conditions:

Competencies are things that companys execute well across several business units or product sectors.

Firms usually have few competencies, but these are usually less liable to change rapidly.

1. It provides consumer benefits
2. It is not easy for competitors to imitate
3. It can be leveraged widely to many products and markets.

A _____ can take various forms, including technical/subject matter know-how, a reliable process and/or close relationships with customers and suppliers (Mascarenhas et al. 1998.)

a. Dominant Design
b. NAIRU
c. Learning-by-doing
d. Core competency

Chapter 7. Strategic Management

21. _____ refers to the stock of skills and knowledge embodied in the ability to perform labor so as to produce economic value. It is the skills and knowledge gained by a worker through education and experience. Many early economic theories refer to it simply as labor, one of three factors of production, and consider it to be a fungible resource -- homogeneous and easily interchangeable.

    a. Market structure
    c. Deflation
    b. Productivity management
    d. Human capital

22. A _____ is a process in which a potential employee is evaluated by an employer for prospective employment in their company, organization and was established in the late 16th century.

A _____ typically precedes the hiring decision, and is used to evaluate the candidate. The interview is usually preceded by the evaluation of submitted résumés from interested candidates, then selecting a small number of candidates for interviews.

    a. Job interview
    c. Split shift
    b. Payrolling
    d. Supported employment

23. The _____ Automobile Company is an automobile manufacturer based in Wolfsburg, Germany, and is the original brand within the _____ Group, as well as the largest brand by sales volume.

_____ means 'people's car' in German, in which it is pronounced . Its current tagline or slogan is Das Auto .

    a. Rate of return
    c. Volkswagen
    b. Turnover
    d. Competence-based Strategic Management

24. The 'business case for _____', theorizes that in a global marketplace, a company that employs a diverse workforce (both men and women, people of many generations, people from ethnically and racially diverse backgrounds etc.) is better able to understand the demographics of the marketplace it serves and is thus better equipped to thrive in that marketplace than a company that has a more limited range of employee demographics.

An additional corollary suggests that a company that supports the _____ of its workforce can also improve employee satisfaction, productivity and retention.

    a. Virtual team
    c. Trademark
    b. Diversity
    d. Kanban

25. In microeconomics and management, the term _____ describes a style of management control. Vertically integrated companies are united through a hierarchy with a common owner. Usually each member of the hierarchy produces a different product or (market-specific) service, and the products combine to satisfy a common need.

    a. 28-hour day
    c. 1990 Clean Air Act
    b. 33 Strategies of War
    d. Vertical integration

26. The phrase mergers and _____s refers to the aspect of corporate strategy, corporate finance and management dealing with the buying, selling and combining of different companies that can aid, finance, or help a growing company in a given industry grow rapidly without having to create another business entity.

An _____, also known as a takeover or a buyout, is the buying of one company (the 'target') by another. An _____ may be friendly or hostile.

  a. AAAI
  b. A Stake in the Outcome
  c. Acquisition
  d. A4e

27. _____ is the corporate management term for the act of reorganizing the legal, ownership, operational, or other structures of a company for the purpose of making it more profitable, or better organized for its present needs. Alternate reasons for _____ include a change of ownership or ownership structure, demerger repositioning debt _____ and financial _____.

  a. Net worth
  b. Restructuring
  c. Market value
  d. Market value added

28. _____ has been described as the 'process of social influence in which one person can enlist the aid and support of others in the accomplishment of a common task' . A definition more inclusive of followers comes from Alan Keith of Genentech who said '_____ is ultimately about creating a way for people to contribute to making something extraordinary happen.'

_____ is one of the most salient aspects of the organizational context. However, defining _____ has been challenging.

  a. 28-hour day
  b. 1990 Clean Air Act
  c. Leadership
  d. Situational leadership

29. _____ is one of the managerial functions like planning, organizing, staffing and directing. It is an important function because it helps to check the errors and to take the corrective action so that deviation from standards are minimized and stated goals of the organization are achieved in desired manner.According to modern concepts, _____ is a foreseeing action whereas earlier concept of _____ was used only when errors were detected. _____ in management means setting standards, measuring actual performance and taking corrective action.

  a. Decision tree pruning
  b. Turnover
  c. Schedule of reinforcement
  d. Control

30. An _____ is a mostly hierarchical concept of subordination of entities that collaborate and contribute to serve one common aim.

Organizations are a variant of clustered entities. The structure of an organization is usually set up in many a styles, dependent on their objectives and ambience.

  a. Open shop
  b. Organizational structure
  c. Organizational development
  d. Informal organization

31. _____ is an increasingly broadening term with which an organization, or other human system describes the combination of traditionally administrative personnel functions with acquisition and application of skills, knowledge and experience, Employee Relations and resource planning at various levels. The field draws upon concepts developed in Industrial/Organizational Psychology and System Theory. _____ has at least two related interpretations depending on context. The original usage derives from political economy and economics, where it was traditionally called labor, one of four factors of production although this perspective is changing as a function of new and ongoing research into more strategic approaches at national levels. This first usage is used more in terms of '_____ development', and can go beyond just organizations to the level of nations. The more traditional usage within corporations and businesses refers to the individuals within a firm or agency, and to the portion of the organization that deals with hiring, firing, training, and other personnel issues, typically referred to as `_____ management'.
   a. Human resources
   b. Progressive discipline
   c. Human resource management
   d. Bradford Factor

32. _____ according to Onuoha (2007) is the practice of starting new organizations or revitalizing mature organizations, particularly new businesses generally in response to identified opportunities. _____ is often a difficult undertaking, as a vast majority of new businesses fail. Entrepreneurial activities are substantially different depending on the type of organization that is being started.
   a. Entrepreneurship
   b. AAAI
   c. A Stake in the Outcome
   d. A4e

Chapter 8. Entrepreneurship and Innovation

1. An _____ is a person who has possession of an enterprise and assumes significant accountability for the inherent risks and the outcome. It is an ambitious leader who combines land, labor, and capital to create and market new goods or services. The term is a loanword from French and was first defined by the Irish economist Richard Cantillon.
   a. A Stake in the Outcome
   b. A4e
   c. AAAI
   d. Entrepreneur

2. _____ according to Onuoha (2007) is the practice of starting new organizations or revitalizing mature organizations, particularly new businesses generally in response to identified opportunities. _____ is often a difficult undertaking, as a vast majority of new businesses fail. Entrepreneurial activities are substantially different depending on the type of organization that is being started.
   a. A4e
   b. Entrepreneurship
   c. AAAI
   d. A Stake in the Outcome

3. A _____ is a business that is privately owned and operated, with a small number of employees and relatively low volume of sales. The legal definition of 'small' often varies by country and industry, but is generally under 100 employees in the United States and under 50 employees in the European Union. In comparison, the definition of mid-sized business by the number of employees is generally under 500 in the U.S. and 250 for the European Union.
   a. Small business
   b. Critical Success Factor
   c. Pre-determined overhead rate
   d. Golden Boot Compensation

4. _____ is a term defined by the Oxford English Dictionary as an individual's 'course or progress through life '. It is usually considered to pertain to remunerative work (and sometimes also formal education.)

   The etymology of the term is somewhat ironic in that it comes from the Latin word carrera, which means race .

   a. Nursing shortage
   b. Spatial mismatch
   c. Career planning
   d. Career

5. _____ is the strategic and coherent approach to the management of an organisation's most valued assets - the people working there who individually and collectively contribute to the achievement of the objectives of the business. The terms '_____' and 'human resources' (HR) have largely replaced the term 'personnel management' as a description of the processes involved in managing people in organizations. In simple sense, _____ means employing people, developing their resources, utilizing, maintaining and compensating their services in tune with the job and organizational requirement.
   a. Human resource management
   b. Progressive discipline
   c. Job knowledge
   d. Revolving door syndrome

6. In organizational development (or OD), the study of _____ looks at:

   - how individuals manage their careers within and between organizations
   - and how organizations structure the career progress of their members, it can also be tied into succession planning within some organizations.

In personal development, _____ is:

- '... the total constellation of psychological, sociological, educational, physical, economic, and chance factors that combine to influence the nature and significance of work in the total lifespan of any given individual.'

- '... the lifelong psychological and behavioral processes as well as contextual influences shaping one's career over the life span. As such, _____ involves the person's creation of a career pattern, decision-making style, integration of life roles, values expression, and life-role self concepts.'

Figures in _____

- Jeff A. Brown
- Jesse B. Davis
- Caela Farren
- John L. Holland
- Kris Magnusson
- Frank Parsons
- Vance Peavy
- Edgar Schein
- Rino Schreuder
- Mark L. Savickas
- Donald Super

a. Horizontal integration
b. Sole proprietorship
c. Business process reengineering
d. Career development

7. _____ is a process of planning and controlling the performance or execution of any type of activity, such as:

- a project (project _____) or
- a process (process _____, sometimes referred to as the process performance measurement and management system.)

Organization's senior management is responsible for carrying out its _____.

a. Participatory management
b. Human Relations Movement
c. Work design
d. Management process

8. _____ is a mathematical science pertaining to the collection, analysis, interpretation or explanation, and presentation of data. It also provides tools for prediction and forecasting based on data. It is applicable to a wide variety of academic disciplines, from the natural and social sciences to the humanities, government and business.

a. Simple moving average
b. Location parameter
c. Failure rate
d. Statistics

9. The 'business case for _____', theorizes that in a global marketplace, a company that employs a diverse workforce (both men and women, people of many generations, people from ethnically and racially diverse backgrounds etc.) is better able to understand the demographics of the marketplace it serves and is thus better equipped to thrive in that marketplace than a company that has a more limited range of employee demographics.

An additional corollary suggests that a company that supports the _____ of its workforce can also improve employee satisfaction, productivity and retention.

a. Diversity
b. Trademark
c. Virtual team
d. Kanban

10.

The terms _____ and positive action refer to policies that take race, ethnicity, or gender into consideration in an attempt to promote equal opportunity. The focus of such policies ranges from employment and education to public contracting and health programs. The impetus towards _____ is twofold: to maximize diversity in all levels of society, along with its presumed benefits, and to redress perceived disadvantages due to overt, institutional, or involuntary discrimination.

a. Affirmative action
b. Affiliation
c. Abraham Harold Maslow
d. Adam Smith

11. _____ is a term in psychology which refers to a person's belief about what causes the good or bad results in his or her life, either in general or in a specific area such as health or academics. Understanding of the concept was developed by Julian B. Rotter in 1954, and has since become an important aspect of personality studies.

_____ refers to the extent to which individuals believe that they can control events that affect them.

a. Social loafing
b. Self-enhancement
c. Machiavellianism
d. Locus of control

12. _____ is one of the managerial functions like planning, organizing, staffing and directing. It is an important function because it helps to check the errors and to take the corrective action so that deviation from standards are minimized and stated goals of the organization are achieved in desired manner. According to modern concepts, _____ is a foreseeing action whereas earlier concept of _____ was used only when errors were detected. _____ in management means setting standards, measuring actual performance and taking corrective action.

a. Decision tree pruning
b. Turnover
c. Schedule of reinforcement
d. Control

13. _____ is a marketing method by which business opportunities are created through networks of like-minded business people. There are several prominent _____ organizations that create models of networking activity that, when followed, allow the business person to build new business relationship and generate business opportunities at the same time.

Chapter 8. Entrepreneurship and Innovation

Many business people contend _____ is a more cost-effective method of generating new business than advertising or public relations efforts.

a. Business networking
c. Cross-selling
b. Business model design
d. Yield management

14. _____ has been described as the 'process of social influence in which one person can enlist the aid and support of others in the accomplishment of a common task'. A definition more inclusive of followers comes from Alan Keith of Genentech who said '_____ is ultimately about creating a way for people to contribute to making something extraordinary happen.'

_____ is one of the most salient aspects of the organizational context. However, defining _____ has been challenging.

a. Situational leadership
c. Leadership
b. 28-hour day
d. 1990 Clean Air Act

15. A _____ is a formal statement of a set of business goals, the reasons why they are believed attainable, and the plan for reaching those goals. It may also contain background information about the organization or team attempting to reach those goals.

The business goals may be defined for for-profit or for non-profit organizations.

a. Time management
c. Distributed management
b. Crisis management
d. Business plan

16. A _____ is a type of business entity in which partners (owners) share with each other the profits or losses of the business. _____s are often favored over corporations for taxation purposes, as the _____ structure does not generally incur a tax on profits before it is distributed to the partners (i.e. there is no dividend tax levied.) However, depending on the _____ structure and the jurisdiction in which it operates, owners of a _____ may be exposed to greater personal liability than they would as shareholders of a corporation.

a. Due process
c. Federal Employers Liability Act
b. Mediation
d. Partnership

17. A _____ also known as a sole trader, or simply proprietorship is a type of business entity which there is only one owner and he has the final word taking all desicions by himself. All debts of the business are debts of the owner and must pay from his personal possessions. This means that the owner has unlimited liabilty.

a. Foreign ownership
c. Golden hello
b. Business rule
d. Sole proprietorship

18. _____ is a legally declared inability or impairment of ability of an individual or organization to pay its creditors. Creditors may file a _____ petition against a debtor ('involuntary _____') in an effort to recoup a portion of what they are owed or initiate a restructuring. In the majority of cases, however, _____ is initiated by the debtor (a 'voluntary _____' that is filed by the insolvent individual or organization.)

Chapter 8. Entrepreneurship and Innovation

a. 33 Strategies of War
b. 28-hour day
c. 1990 Clean Air Act
d. Bankruptcy

19. A _____ is a person or investment firm that makes venture investments, and these _____s are expected to bring managerial and technical expertise as well as capital to their investments. A venture capital fund refers to a pooled investment vehicle that primarily invests the financial capital of third-party investors in enterprises that are too risky for the standard capital markets or bank loans.

Venture capital is also associated with job creation, the knowledge economy and used as a proxy measure of innovation within an economic sector or geography.

a. Limited partners
b. Private equity
c. Limited liability corporation
d. Venture capitalist

20. _____ , also referred to simply as a 'public offering' or 'flotation,' is when a company issues common stock or shares to the public for the first time. They are often issued by smaller, younger companies seeking capital to expand, but can also be done by large privately-owned companies looking to become publicly traded.

In an _____ the issuer may obtain the assistance of an underwriting firm, which helps it determine what type of security to issue (common or preferred), best offering price and time to bring it to market.

a. Unemployment insurance
b. Initial public offering
c. Occupational Safety and Health Administration
d. Outsourcing

21. _____ is the practice of using entrepreneurial skills without taking on the risks or accountability associated with entrepreneurial activities. It is practiced by employees within an established organization using a business model. Employees, perhaps engaged in a special project within a larger firm are supposed to behave as entrepreneurs, even though they have the resources and capabilities of the larger firm to draw upon.

a. A Stake in the Outcome
b. A4e
c. AAAI
d. Intrapreneurship

22. A _____ is a new organization or entity formed by a split from a larger one, such as a television series based on a pre-existing one, or a new company formed from a university research group or business incubator. In literature, especially in milieu-based popular fictional book series like mysteries, westerns, fantasy or science fiction, the term sub-series is generally used instead of _____, but with essentially the same meaning.

_____s as a descriptive term can also include a dissenting faction of a membership organization, a sect of a cult, or a denomination of a church.

a. 28-hour day
b. Spin-off
c. 33 Strategies of War
d. 1990 Clean Air Act

Chapter 8. Entrepreneurship and Innovation

23. Procter is a surname, and may also refer to:

- Bryan Waller Procter (pseud. Barry Cornwall), English poet
- Goodwin Procter, American law firm
- _____, consumer products multinational

a. Master and Servant Acts
c. Strict liability

b. Downstream
d. Procter ' Gamble

24. _____ is the discipline of managing processes in research and development (R'D) and innovation. It can be used to develop both product and organizational innovation. Without proper processes, it is not possible for R'D to be efficient; _____ includes a set of tools that allow managers and engineers to cooperate with a common understanding of goals and processes.

a. A4e
c. AAAI

b. A Stake in the Outcome
d. Innovation Management

25. _____ is an idea in the field of Organizational studies and management which describes the psychology, attitudes, experiences, beliefs and Values (personal and cultural values) of an organization. It has been defined as 'the specific collection of values and norms that are shared by people and groups in an organization and that control the way they interact with each other and with stakeholders outside the organization.'

This definition continues to explain organizational values also known as 'beliefs and ideas about what kinds of goals members of an organization should pursue and ideas about the appropriate kinds or standards of behavior organizational members should use to achieve these goals. From organizational values develop organizational norms, guidelines or expectations that prescribe appropriate kinds of behavior by employees in particular situations and control the behavior of organizational members towards one another.'

_____ is not the same as corporate culture.

a. Organizational effectiveness
c. Organizational development

b. Union shop
d. Organizational culture

26. _____ is, in very basic words, a position a firm occupies against its competitors.

According to Michael Porter, the three methods for creating a sustainable _____ are through:

1. Cost leadership

2. Differentiation

3. Focus (economics)

a. Theory Z
b. Competitive advantage
c. 28-hour day
d. 1990 Clean Air Act

27. _____ refers to the methods of practicing and using another person's business philosophy. The franchisor grants the independent operator the right to distribute its products, techniques, and trademarks for a percentage of gross monthly sales and a royalty fee. Various tangibles and intangibles such as national or international advertising, training, and other support services are commonly made available by the franchisor.

a. 28-hour day
b. 1990 Clean Air Act
c. ServiceMaster
d. Franchising

28. _____ is an advertisement in which a particular product specifically mentions a competitor by name for the express purpose of showing why the competitor is inferior to the product naming it.

This should not be confused with parody advertisements, where a fictional product is being advertised for the purpose of poking fun at the particular advertisement, nor should it be confused with the use of a coined brand name for the purpose of comparing the product without actually naming an actual competitor. ('Wikipedia tastes better and is less filling than the Encyclopedia Galactica.')

In the 1980s, during what has been referred to as the cola wars, soft-drink manufacturer Pepsi ran a series of advertisements where people, caught on hidden camera, in a blind taste test, chose Pepsi over rival Coca-Cola.

a. 28-hour day
b. 33 Strategies of War
c. Comparative advertising
d. 1990 Clean Air Act

Chapter 9. Managing the Structure and Design of Organizations

1. _____ is a concept in ethics with several meanings. It is often used synonymously with such concepts as responsibility, answerability, enforcement, blameworthiness, liability and other terms associated with the expectation of account-giving. As an aspect of governance, it has been central to discussions related to problems in both the public and private (corporation) worlds.

   a. Usury
   b. A Stake in the Outcome
   c. A4e
   d. Accountability

2. The _____ is a standardized, on-scene, all-hazard incident management concept. It is a management protocol originally designed for emergency management agencies in the United States which was later federalized there. It has since been adopted by agencies in other countries.

   a. AAAI
   b. A Stake in the Outcome
   c. A4e
   d. Incident Command Structure

3. In a military context, the _____ is the line of authority and responsibility along which orders are passed within a military unit and between different units. The term is also used in a civilian management context describing comparable hierarchical structures of authority.

   a. 28-hour day
   b. Chain of command
   c. French leave
   d. 1990 Clean Air Act

4. _____ is a process of agreeing upon objectives within an organization so that management and employees agree to the objectives and understand what they are in the organization.

   The term '_____' was first popularized by Peter Drucker in his 1954 book 'The Practice of Management'.

   The essence of _____ is participative goal setting, choosing course of actions and decision making.

   a. Clean sheet review
   b. Business economics
   c. Job enrichment
   d. Management by objectives

5. An _____, or organogram(me)) is a diagram that shows the structure of an organization and the relationships and relative ranks of its parts and positions/jobs. The term is also used for similar diagrams, for example ones showing the different elements of a field of knowledge or a group of languages. The French Encyclopédie had one of the first _____s of knowledge in general.

   a. A4e
   b. AAAI
   c. A Stake in the Outcome
   d. Organizational chart

6. _____ is a term originating in military organization theory, but now used more commonly in business management, particularly human resource management. _____ refers to the number of subordinates a supervisor has.

   In the hierarchical business organization of the past it was not uncommon to see average spans of 1 to 10 or even less. That is, one manager supervised ten employees on average.

   a. Span of control
   b. Senior management
   c. Mentoring
   d. CIFMS

Chapter 9. Managing the Structure and Design of Organizations

7. _____ is one of the managerial functions like planning, organizing, staffing and directing. It is an important function because it helps to check the errors and to take the corrective action so that deviation from standards are minimized and stated goals of the organization are achieved in desired manner. According to modern concepts, _____ is a foreseeing action whereas earlier concept of _____ was used only when errors were detected. _____ in management means setting standards, measuring actual performance and taking corrective action.

   a. Schedule of reinforcement
   b. Control
   c. Decision tree pruning
   d. Turnover

8. _____ is the process by which the activities of an organisation, particularly those regarding decision-making, become concentrated within a particular location and/or group.

   a. Corner office
   b. Centralization
   c. Product innovation
   d. Chief operating officer

9. _____ is the process of dispersing decision-making governance closer to the people or citizen. It includes the dispersal of administration or governance in sectors or areas like engineering, management science, political science, political economy, sociology and economics. _____ is also possible in the dispersal of population and employment.

   a. Business plan
   b. Frenemy
   c. Formula for Change
   d. Decentralization

10. _____ refers to the process of grouping activities into departments.

    Division of labour creates specialists who need coordination. This coordination is facilitated by grouping specialists together in departments.

    a. Decent work
    b. Division of labour
    c. Departmentalization
    d. Maximum wage

11. _____ is the strategic and coherent approach to the management of an organisation's most valued assets - the people working there who individually and collectively contribute to the achievement of the objectives of the business. The terms '_____' and 'human resources' (HR) have largely replaced the term 'personnel management' as a description of the processes involved in managing people in organizations. In simple sense, _____ means employing people, developing their resources, utilizing, maintaining and compensating their services in tune with the job and organizational requirement.

    a. Revolving door syndrome
    b. Progressive discipline
    c. Job knowledge
    d. Human resource management

12. Procter is a surname, and may also refer to:

    - Bryan Waller Procter (pseud. Barry Cornwall), English poet
    - Goodwin Procter, American law firm
    - _____, consumer products multinational

    a. Downstream
    b. Procter ' Gamble
    c. Strict liability
    d. Master and Servant Acts

Chapter 9. Managing the Structure and Design of Organizations 57

13. _____ is a term defined by the Oxford English Dictionary as an individual's 'course or progress through life '. It is usually considered to pertain to remunerative work (and sometimes also formal education.)

The etymology of the term is somewhat ironic in that it comes from the Latin word carrera, which means race .

a. Nursing shortage
c. Career planning
b. Career
d. Spatial mismatch

14. In organizational development (or OD), the study of _____ looks at:

- how individuals manage their careers within and between organizations
- and how organizations structure the career progress of their members, it can also be tied into succession planning within some organizations.

In personal development, _____ is:

- ' ... the total constellation of psychological, sociological, educational, physical, economic, and chance factors that combine to influence the nature and significance of work in the total lifespan of any given individual.'

- '... the lifelong psychological and behavioral processes as well as contextual influences shaping one's career over the life span. As such, _____ involves the person's creation of a career pattern, decision-making style, integration of life roles, values expression, and life-role self concepts.'

Figures in _____

- Jeff A. Brown
- Jesse B. Davis
- Caela Farren
- John L. Holland
- Kris Magnusson
- Frank Parsons
- Vance Peavy
- Edgar Schein
- Rino Schreuder
- Mark L. Savickas
- Donald Super

a. Business process reengineering
c. Horizontal integration
b. Sole proprietorship
d. Career development

Chapter 9. Managing the Structure and Design of Organizations

15. _____ is a process of planning and controlling the performance or execution of any type of activity, such as:

- a project (project _____) or
- a process (process _____, sometimes referred to as the process performance measurement and management system.)

Organization's senior management is responsible for carrying out its _____.

a. Work design
c. Human Relations Movement
b. Participatory management
d. Management process

16. _____ can be regarded as an outcome of mental processes (cognitive process) leading to the selection of a course of action among several alternatives. Every _____ process produces a final choice. The output can be an action or an opinion of choice.

a. 28-hour day
c. 1990 Clean Air Act
b. 33 Strategies of War
d. Decision making

17. In neuroscience, the _____ is a collection of brain structures which attempts to regulate and control behavior by inducing pleasurable effects.

A psychological reward is a process that reinforces behavior -- something that, when offered, causes a behavior to increase in intensity. Reward is an operational concept for describing the positive value an individual ascribes to an object, behavioral act or an internal physical state.

a. 1990 Clean Air Act
c. 28-hour day
b. 33 Strategies of War
d. Reward system

18. A _____ is a name or trademark connected with a product or producer. _____s have become increasingly important components of culture and the economy, now being described as 'cultural accessories and personal philosophies'.

Some people distinguish the psychological aspect of a _____ from the experiential aspect.

a. Brand loyalty
c. Brand extension
b. Brand awareness
d. Brand

19. _____ is an idea in the field of Organizational studies and management which describes the psychology, attitudes, experiences, beliefs and Values (personal and cultural values) of an organization. It has been defined as 'the specific collection of values and norms that are shared by people and groups in an organization and that control the way they interact with each other and with stakeholders outside the organization.'

This definition continues to explain organizational values also known as 'beliefs and ideas about what kinds of goals members of an organization should pursue and ideas about the appropriate kinds or standards of behavior organizational members should use to achieve these goals. From organizational values develop organizational norms, guidelines or expectations that prescribe appropriate kinds of behavior by employees in particular situations and control the behavior of organizational members towards one another.'

Chapter 9. Managing the Structure and Design of Organizations

_____ is not the same as corporate culture.

a. Union shop
c. Organizational effectiveness
b. Organizational development
d. Organizational culture

20. _____ refers to the movement of cash into or out of a business or financial product. It is usually measured during a specified, finite period of time. Measurement of _____ can be used

- to determine a project's rate of return or value. The time of _____s into and out of projects are used as inputs in financial models such as internal rate of return, and net present value.
- to determine problems with a business's liquidity. Being profitable does not necessarily mean being liquid. A company can fail because of a shortage of cash, even while profitable.
- as an alternate measure of a business's profits when it is believed that accrual accounting concepts do not represent economic realities. For example, a company may be notionally profitable but generating little operational cash (as may be the case for a company that barters its products rather than selling for cash.) In such a case, the company may be deriving additional operating cash by issuing shares evaluating default risk, re-investment requirements, etc.

_____ is a generic term used differently depending on the context. It may be defined by users for their own purposes.

a. Gross profit margin
c. Gross profit
b. Sweat equity
d. Cash flow

21. A _____ is a professional in the field of project management. _____s can have the responsibility of the planning, execution, and closing of any project, typically relating to construction industry, architecture, computer networking, telecommunications or software development.

Many other fields in the production, design and service industries also have _____s.

a. Work package
c. Project management
b. Project engineer
d. Project manager

22. A _____ is a contemporary apporach to organizational design. It is an organization that is not defined by, or limited to, the horizontal, vertical, or external boundaries imposed by a predefined structure. This term was coined by former GE chairman Jack Welch because he wanted to eliminate vertical and horizontal boundaries within GE and break down external barriers between the company and its customers and suppliers.

a. Headquarters
c. Chief risk officer
b. Boundaryless organization
d. Business Roundtable

23. A _____ is a formal relationship between two or more parties to pursue a set of agreed upon goals or to meet a critical business need while remaining independent organizations.

Partners may provide the _____ with resources such as products, distribution channels, manufacturing capability, project funding, capital equipment, knowledge, expertise, or intellectual property. The alliance is a cooperation or collaboration which aims for a synergy where each partner hopes that the benefits from the alliance will be greater than those from individual efforts.

a. Process automation
b. Strategic alliance
c. Golden parachute
d. Farmshoring

24. The phrase mergers and _____s refers to the aspect of corporate strategy, corporate finance and management dealing with the buying, selling and combining of different companies that can aid, finance, or help a growing company in a given industry grow rapidly without having to create another business entity.

An _____, also known as a takeover or a buyout, is the buying of one company (the 'target') by another. An _____ may be friendly or hostile.

a. A Stake in the Outcome
b. A4e
c. Acquisition
d. AAAI

25. In finance and economics, _____ or divestiture is the reduction of some kind of asset for either financial or ethical objectives or sale of an existing business by a firm. A _____ is the opposite of an investment.

a. 28-hour day
b. Divestment
c. 1990 Clean Air Act
d. 33 Strategies of War

26. _____ is a diversified financial services company with operations around the world. Wells Fargo is the fourth largest bank in the US by assets and the second largest bank by market cap.

a. Committee for Economic Development
b. Holding company
c. Process-based management
d. Wells Fargo ' Co.

Chapter 10. Human Resources Management

1. _____ is the strategic and coherent approach to the management of an organisation's most valued assets - the people working there who individually and collectively contribute to the achievement of the objectives of the business. The terms '_____' and 'human resources' (HR) have largely replaced the term 'personnel management' as a description of the processes involved in managing people in organizations. In simple sense, _____ means employing people, developing their resources, utilizing, maintaining and compensating their services in tune with the job and organizational requirement.
   a. Revolving door syndrome
   b. Job knowledge
   c. Human resource management
   d. Progressive discipline

2. _____ is a term defined by the Oxford English Dictionary as an individual's 'course or progress through life '. It is usually considered to pertain to remunerative work (and sometimes also formal education.)

   The etymology of the term is somewhat ironic in that it comes from the Latin word carrera, which means race .

   a. Spatial mismatch
   b. Career planning
   c. Nursing shortage
   d. Career

3. In organizational development (or OD), the study of _____ looks at:

   - how individuals manage their careers within and between organizations
   - and how organizations structure the career progress of their members, it can also be tied into succession planning within some organizations.

   In personal development, _____ is:

   - ' ... the total constellation of psychological, sociological, educational, physical, economic, and chance factors that combine to influence the nature and significance of work in the total lifespan of any given individual.'

   - '... the lifelong psychological and behavioral processes as well as contextual influences shaping one's career over the life span. As such, _____ involves the person's creation of a career pattern, decision-making style, integration of life roles, values expression, and life-role self concepts.'

Figures in _____

- Jeff A. Brown
- Jesse B. Davis
- Caela Farren
- John L. Holland
- Kris Magnusson
- Frank Parsons
- Vance Peavy
- Edgar Schein
- Rino Schreuder
- Mark L. Savickas
- Donald Super

a. Business process reengineering
c. Sole proprietorship
b. Career development
d. Horizontal integration

4. _____ is a process of planning and controlling the performance or execution of any type of activity, such as:

- a project (project _____) or
- a process (process _____, sometimes referred to as the process performance measurement and management system.)

Organization's senior management is responsible for carrying out its _____.

a. Human Relations Movement
c. Work design
b. Participatory management
d. Management process

5. A _____ is a list of the general tasks and responsibilities of a position. Typically, it also includes to whom the position reports, specifications such as the qualifications needed by the person in the job, salary range for the position, etc. A _____ is usually developed by conducting a job analysis, which includes examining the tasks and sequences of tasks necessary to perform the job.

a. Recruitment Process Insourcing
c. Recruitment advertising
b. Recruitment
d. Job description

Chapter 10. Human Resources Management

6. _____ is an increasingly broadening term with which an organization, or other human system describes the combination of traditionally administrative personnel functions with acquisition and application of skills, knowledge and experience, Employee Relations and resource planning at various levels. The field draws upon concepts developed in Industrial/Organizational Psychology and System Theory. _____ has at least two related interpretations depending on context. The original usage derives from political economy and economics, where it was traditionally called labor, one of four factors of production although this perspective is changing as a function of new and ongoing research into more strategic approaches at national levels. This first usage is used more in terms of '_____ development', and can go beyond just organizations to the level of nations . The more traditional usage within corporations and businesses refers to the individuals within a firm or agency, and to the portion of the organization that deals with hiring, firing, training, and other personnel issues, typically referred to as `_____ management'.
   - a. Bradford Factor
   - b. Progressive discipline
   - c. Human resource management
   - d. Human resources

7. The 'business case for _____', theorizes that in a global marketplace, a company that employs a diverse workforce (both men and women, people of many generations, people from ethnically and racially diverse backgrounds etc.) is better able to understand the demographics of the marketplace it serves and is thus better equipped to thrive in that marketplace than a company that has a more limited range of employee demographics.

   An additional corollary suggests that a company that supports the _____ of its workforce can also improve employee satisfaction, productivity and retention.

   - a. Diversity
   - b. Virtual team
   - c. Trademark
   - d. Kanban

8. _____ in its literal sense is the process of transformation of local or regional phenomena into global ones. It can be described as a process by which the people of the world are unified into a single society and function together.

   This process is a combination of economic, technological, sociocultural and political forces.

   - a. Collaborative Planning, Forecasting and Replenishment
   - b. Histogram
   - c. Cost Management
   - d. Globalization

9. The _____ is the labour pool in employment. It is generally used to describe those working for a single company or industry, but can also apply to a geographic region like a city, country, state, etc. The term generally excludes the employers or management, and implies those involved in manual labour.
   - a. Work-life balance
   - b. Pink-collar worker
   - c. Division of labour
   - d. Workforce

10.

The terms _____ and positive action refer to policies that take race, ethnicity, or gender into consideration in an attempt to promote equal opportunity. The focus of such policies ranges from employment and education to public contracting and health programs. The impetus towards _____ is twofold: to maximize diversity in all levels of society, along with its presumed benefits, and to redress perceived disadvantages due to overt, institutional, or involuntary discrimination.

a. Affiliation
b. Abraham Harold Maslow
c. Adam Smith
d. Affirmative action

11. An _____ is a person who has possession of an enterprise and assumes significant accountability for the inherent risks and the outcome. It is an ambitious leader who combines land, labor, and capital to create and market new goods or services. The term is a loanword from French and was first defined by the Irish economist Richard Cantillon.
   a. A Stake in the Outcome
   b. Entrepreneur
   c. A4e
   d. AAAI

12. The _____ was a landmark piece of legislation in the United States that outlawed racial segregation in schools, public places, and employment.
   a. Design patent
   b. Financial Security Law of France
   c. Civil Rights Act of 1964
   d. Negligence in employment

13. In US employment law, _____ is defined as a substantially different rate of selection in hiring, promotion sex statistical significance tests, and/or practical significance tests. _____ is often used interchangeably with 'disparate impact,' which was a legal term coined in one of the most significant U.S. Supreme Court rulings on disparate or _____: Griggs v. Duke Power Co., 1971.
   a. AAAI
   b. A4e
   c. A Stake in the Outcome
   d. Adverse impact

14. _____ is a contract between two parties, one being the employer and the other being the employee. An employee may be defined as: 'A person in the service of another under any contract of hire, express or implied, oral or written, where the employer has the power or right to control and direct the employee in the material details of how the work is to be performed.' Black's Law Dictionary page 471 (5th ed. 1979.)
   a. Employment counsellor
   b. Employment rate
   c. Exit interview
   d. Employment

15. The term _____ was created by President Lyndon B. Johnson when he signed Executive Order 11246 on September 24, 1965, created to prohibit federal contractors from discriminating against employees on the basis of race, sex, creed, religion, color, or national origin. In more recent times, most employers have also added sexual orientation to the list of non-discrimination.

The Executive Order also required contractors to implement affirmative action plans to increase the participation of minorities and women in the workplace.

   a. AAAI
   b. A4e
   c. A Stake in the Outcome
   d. Equal Employment Opportunity

16. The U.S. _____ is a federal agency whose goal is ending employment discrimination. The _____ investigates discrimination complaints based on an individual's race, color, national origin, religion, sex, age, disability and retaliation for reporting and/or opposing a discriminatory practice. The Commission is also tasked with filing suits on behalf of alleged victim(s) of discrimination against employers and as an adjudicatory for claims of discrimination brought against federal agencies.

Chapter 10. Human Resources Management

a. ARCO
b. Airbus SAS
c. Airbus Industrie
d. Equal Employment Opportunity Commission

17. A _____ is one scenario provided for evaluation by respondents in a Choice Experiment. Responses are collected and used to create a Choice Model. Respondents are usually provided with a series of differing _____s for evaluation.
a. Choice Set
b. Computerized classification test
c. Thurstone scale
d. Pairwise comparison

18. In employment law, a (BFOQ) (US) or bona fide occupational requirement (BFOR) (Canada) is a quality or an attribute that employers are allowed to consider when making decisions on the hiring and retention of employees - qualities that, when considered, in other contexts would be considered discriminatory and thus violating civil rights employment law.

In employment discrimination law in the United States, United States Code Title 29 , Chapter 14 (age discrimination in employment), section 623 (prohibition of age discrimination) establishes that 'It shall not be unlawful for an employer, employment agency, or labor organization (1) to take any action otherwise prohibited under subsections (a), (b), (c), or (e) of this section where age is a _____ reasonably necessary to the normal operation of the particular business, or where the differentiation is based on reasonable factors other than age, or where such practices involve an employee in a workplace in a foreign country, and compliance with such subsections would cause such employer, or a corporation controlled by such employer, to violate the laws of the country in which such workplace is located.'

One example of _____s are mandatory retirement ages for bus drivers and airline pilots, for safety reasons. Further, in advertising, a manufacturer of men's clothing may lawfully advertise for male models.

a. Bona fide occupational qualification
b. Corporate governance
c. Sick leave
d. MacPherson v. Buick Motor Co.

19. The _____ is a United States labor law allowing an employee to take unpaid leave due to a serious health condition that makes the employee unable to perform his job or to care for a sick family member or to care for a new son or daughter (including by birth, adoption or foster care.) The bill was among the first signed into law by President Bill Clinton in his first term.
a. Contributory negligence
b. Harvester Judgment
c. Sarbanes-Oxley Act of 2002
d. Family and Medical Leave Act of 1993

20. _____ describes the situation when output from (or information about the result of) an event or phenomenon in the past will influence the same event/phenomenon in the present or future. When an event is part of a chain of cause-and-effect that forms a circuit or loop, then the event is said to 'feed back' into itself.

_____ is also a synonym for:

- _____ signal; the information about the initial event that is the basis for subsequent modification of the event.
- _____ loop; the causal path that leads from the initial generation of the _____ signal to the subsequent modification of the event.

_____ is a mechanism, process or signal that is looped back to control a system within itself. Such a loop is called a _____ loop.

a. Feedback
c. 1990 Clean Air Act
b. Feedback loop
d. Positive feedback

21. _____ indicates a more-or-less equal exchange or substitution of goods or services. English speakers often use the term to mean 'a favour for a favour' and the phrases with almost identical meaning include: 'what for what,' 'give and take,' 'tit for tat', 'this for that', and 'you scratch my back, and I'll scratch yours'.

In legal usage, _____ indicates that an item or a service has been traded in return for something of value, usually when the propriety or equity of the transaction is in question.

a. 33 Strategies of War
c. Quid pro quo
b. 28-hour day
d. 1990 Clean Air Act

22. _____ is the concept of a person or group of people being in charge or in command of another person or group. This control is often granted to the senior person(s) due to experience or length of service in a given position, but it is not uncommon for a senior person(s) to have less experience or length of service than their subordinates.

More generally, '_____' can be a description of an individual's experience or length of service, and can thus be used to differentiate between individuals of otherwise equivalent status without placing them in a hierarchy of direct authority.

a. 1990 Clean Air Act
c. 28-hour day
b. 33 Strategies of War
d. Seniority

23. _____ is unwelcome harassment of a sexual nature, or based upon the receiving party's sex or gender. In some contexts or circumstances, _____ may be illegal. It includes a range of behavior from seemingly mild transgressions and annoyances to actual sexual abuse or sexual assault.

a. 1990 Clean Air Act
c. Hypernorms
b. 28-hour day
d. Sexual harassment

24. _____ is a doctrine of American law that defines an employment relationship in which either party can break the relationship with no liability, provided there was no express contract for a definite term governing the employment relationship and that the employer does not belong to a collective bargain (i.e., a union.) Under this legal doctrine:

Chapter 10. Human Resources Management

Several exceptions to the doctrine exist, especially if unlawful discrimination is involved regarding the termination of an employee.

As a means of downsizing, such as closing an unprofitable factory, a company may terminate employees en masse.

a. AAAI
b. A4e
c. A Stake in the Outcome
d. At-will employment

25. A _____ is a process in which a potential employee is evaluated by an employer for prospective employment in their company, organization and was established in the late 16th century.

A _____ typically precedes the hiring decision, and is used to evaluate the candidate. The interview is usually preceded by the evaluation of submitted résumés from interested candidates, then selecting a small number of candidates for interviews.

a. Payrolling
b. Split shift
c. Job interview
d. Supported employment

26. A _____ or labor union is an organization of workers who have banded together to achieve common goals in key areas and working conditions. The _____, through its leadership, bargains with the employer on behalf of union members (rank and file members) and negotiates labor contracts (Collective bargaining) with employers. This may include the negotiation of wages, work rules, complaint procedures, rules governing hiring, firing and promotion of workers, benefits, workplace safety and policies.

a. Company union
b. Labour law
c. Working time
d. Trade union

27. The term '_____' refers to the concept of collecting information and attempting to spot a pattern in the information. In some fields of study, the term '_____' has more formally-defined meanings.

In project management _____ is a mathematical technique that uses historical results to predict future outcome.

a. Regression analysis
b. Trend analysis
c. Stepwise regression
d. Least squares

28. A _____, business union or, pejoratively, a yellow union is a union which is located within and run by a company, and is not affiliated with an independent trade union (known as a 'red union' in this context.) _____s were outlawed in the United States by the 1935 National Labor Relations Act, due to their use as agents for interference with independent unions, but _____s were and are common in many other countries. Some labor organizations are accused by rival unions of behaving like '_____s' if they are seen as to have too close and cordial a relationship with the employer, even though they may be recognized in their respective jurisdictions as bona fide trade unions.

a. Company union
b. Labour law
c. Labor law
d. Four-day week

Chapter 10. Human Resources Management

29. In organized labor, _____ is the method whereby workers organize together (usually in unions) to meet, converse, and negotiate upon the work conditions with their employers normally resulting in a written contract setting forth the wages, hours, and other conditions to be observed for a stipulated period. It is the practice in which union and company representatives meet to negotiate a new labor contract. In various national labor and employment law contexts, the term _____ takes on a more specific legal meaning. In a broad sense, however, it is the coming together of workers to negotiate their employment.

   a. Collective bargaining   b. Paid time off
   c. Labour law   d. Labor rights

30. _____ is a pejorative term for the practice of hiring more workers than are needed to perform a given job or to adopt work procedures which appear pointless complex and time-consuming merely to employ additional workers. The term 'make-work' is sometimes used as a synonym for _____.

The term '_____' is usually used by management to describe behaviors and rules sought by workers.

   a. Featherbedding   b. Customer satisfaction
   c. Business ecosystem   d. Strategic Alliance

31. The field of _____ looks at the relationship between management and workers, particularly groups of workers represented by a union.

_____ is an important factor in analyzing 'varieties of capitalism', such as neocorporatism, social democracy, and neoliberalism

   a. Overtime   b. Informal organization
   c. Organizational effectiveness   d. Industrial relations

32. _____ is the body of laws, administrative rulings, and precedents which address the legal rights of, and restrictions on, working people and their organizations. As such, it mediates many aspects of the relationship between trade unions, employers and employees. In Canada, employment laws related to unionized workplaces are differentiated from those relating to particular individuals.

   a. Trade union   b. Shift work
   c. Four-day week   d. Labor law

33. The _____ is a United States labor law that regulates labor unions' internal affairs and their officials' relationships with employers.

Enacted in 1959 after revelations of corruption and undemocratic practices in the International Brotherhood of Teamsters, International Longshoremen's Association, United Mine Workers and other unions received wide public attention, the Act requires unions to hold secret elections for local union offices on a regular basis and provides for review by the United States Department of Labor of union members' claims of improper election activity.

Chapter 10. Human Resources Management

Other provisions of the law:

- Bar members of the Communist Party and convicted felons from holding union office.
- Require unions to submit annual financial reports to the DOL.
- Declare that every union officer must act as a fiduciary in handling the assets and conducting the affairs of the union.
- Limit the power of unions to put subordinate bodies in trusteeship, a temporary suspension of democratic processes within a union.
- Provide certain minimum standards before a union may expel or take other disciplinary action against a member of the union.

The LMRDA covers both workers and unions covered by the National Labor Relations Act and workers and unions in the railroad and airline industries, who are covered by the Railway Labor Act. The LMRDA does not, as a general rule, cover public sector employees, who are not covered by either the NLRA or the RLA.

a. Civil Rights Act of 1964
b. Labor Management Reporting and Disclosure Act
c. Right-to-work laws
d. Civil Rights Act of 1875

34. The _____ is a 1935 United States federal law that limits the means with which employers may react to workers in the private sector that organize labor unions, engage in collective bargaining, and take part in strikes and other forms of concerted activity in support of their demands. The Act does not, on the other hand, cover those workers who are covered by the Railway Labor Act, agricultural employees, domestic employees, supervisors, independent contractors and some close relatives of individual employers.

It was in a context of severe economic troubles that the Wagner Act came into effect.

a. 33 Strategies of War
b. National Labor Relations Act
c. 1990 Clean Air Act
d. 28-hour day

35. The American Federation of Labor and Congress of Industrial Organizations, commonly _____, is a national trade union center, the largest federation of unions in the United States, made up of 65 national and international unions (including Canadian), together representing more than 10 million workers. It was formed in 1955 when the AFL and the CIO merged after a long estrangement. From 1955 until 2005, the _____'s member unions represented nearly all unionized workers in the United States.

a. AFL-CIO
b. A4e
c. United Mine Workers
d. A Stake in the Outcome

36. _____ is a class of behavioural theory that claims that there is no best way to organize a corporation, to lead a company, or to make decisions. Instead, the optimal course of action is contingent (dependant) upon the internal and external situation. Several contingency approaches were developed concurrently in the late 1960s.

a. Distributed management
b. Contingency theory
c. Commercial management
d. Capability management

Chapter 10. Human Resources Management

37. In mainstream economic theories, the supply of labor is the number of total hours that workers wish to work at a given real wage rate. Realisticly, the _____ is a fuction of various factors within an economy. For instance, overpopulation increases the number of available workers driving down wages and can result in high unemployment.
   a. Labor supply
   b. 28-hour day
   c. 1990 Clean Air Act
   d. 33 Strategies of War

38. _____ is the temporary suspension or permanent termination of employment of an employee or (more commonly) a group of employees for business reasons, such as the decision that certain positions are no longer necessary or a business slow-down or interruption in work. Originally the term '_____' referred exclusively to a temporary interruption in work, as when factory work cyclically falls off. However, in recent times the term can also refer to the permanent elimination of a position.
   a. Layoff
   b. Wrongful dismissal
   c. Termination of employment
   d. Retirement

39. In economics, _____ is the desire to own something and the ability to pay for it. The term _____ signifies the ability or the willingness to buy a particular commodity at a given point of time.
   a. Demand
   b. 1990 Clean Air Act
   c. 33 Strategies of War
   d. 28-hour day

40. _____ refers to various methodologies for analyzing the requirements of a job.

The general purpose of _____ is to document the requirements of a job and the work performed. Job and task analysis is performed as a basis for later improvements, including: definition of a job domain; describing a job; developing performance appraisals, selection systems, promotion criteria, training needs assessment, and compensation plans.

   a. Work design
   b. Job analysis
   c. Management process
   d. Hersey-Blanchard situational theory

41.

_____ is a commonly used, yet poorly defined concept in industrial and organizational psychology, the branch of psychology that deals with the workplace. It most commonly refers to whether a person performs their job well. Despite the confusion over how it should be exactly defined, performance is an extremely important criterion that relates to organizational outcomes and success.

   a. 28-hour day
   b. 33 Strategies of War
   c. 1990 Clean Air Act
   d. Job performance

42. _____ refers to the process of screening, and selecting qualified people for a job at an organization or firm mid- and large-size organizations and companies often retain professional recruiters or outsource some of the process to _____ agencies. External _____ is the process of attracting and selecting employees from outside the organization.

The _____ industry has four main types of agencies: employment agencies, _____ websites and job search engines, 'headhunters' for executive and professional _____, and in-house _____.

Chapter 10. Human Resources Management

a. Labour hire
b. Recruitment
c. Recruitment Process Outsourcing
d. Referral recruitment

43. In psychometrics, _____ refers to the extent to which a measure represents all facets of a given social construct. For example, a depression scale may lack _____ if it only assesses the affective dimension of depression but fails to take into account the behavioral dimension. An element of subjectivity exists in relation to determining _____, which requires a degree of agreement about what a particular personality trait such as extraversion represents.
a. Content validity
b. 28-hour day
c. 33 Strategies of War
d. 1990 Clean Air Act

44. The term _____ in logic applies to arguments or statements.

An argument is valid if and only if the truth of its premises entails the truth of its conclusion, it would be self-contradictory to affirm the premises and deny the conclusion. The corresponding conditional of a valid argument is a logical truth and the negation of its corresponding conditional is a contradiction.

a. Fuzzy logic
b. Validity
c. 1990 Clean Air Act
d. Simplification

45. _____, commonly known as e-commerce, consists of the buying and selling of products or services over electronic systems such as the Internet and other computer networks. The amount of trade conducted electronically has grown extraordinarily with widespread Internet usage. The use of commerce is conducted in this way, spurring and drawing on innovations in electronic funds transfer, supply chain management, Internet marketing, online transaction processing, electronic data interchange (EDI), inventory management systems, and automated data collection systems.
a. Online shopping
b. A Stake in the Outcome
c. Electronic Commerce
d. A4e

46. _____ is a process for determining and addressing needs, or gaps between current conditions and desired conditions organizations it is known as community needs analysis. It involves identifying material problems/deficits/weaknesses and advantages/opportunites/strengths, and evaluating possible solutions that take those qualities into consideration.
a. 1990 Clean Air Act
b. 33 Strategies of War
c. Needs assessment
d. 28-hour day

47. _____ is a group creativity technique designed to generate a large number of ideas for the solution of a problem. The method was first popularized in the late 1930s by Alex Faickney Osborn in a book called Applied Imagination. Osborn proposed that groups could double their creative output with _____.
a. Affiliation
b. Adam Smith
c. Abraham Harold Maslow
d. Brainstorming

48. _____ is an organization's process of defining its strategy and making decisions on allocating its resources to pursue this strategy, including its capital and people. Various business analysis techniques can be used in _____, including SWOT analysis (Strengths, Weaknesses, Opportunities, and Threats) and PEST analysis (Political, Economic, Social, and Technological analysis) or STEER analysis involving Socio-cultural, Technological, Economic, Ecological, and Regulatory factors and EPISTEL (Environment, Political, Informatic, Social, Technological, Economic and Legal)

Chapter 10. Human Resources Management

_____ is the formal consideration of an organization's future course. All _____ deals with at least one of three key questions:

1. 'What do we do?'
2. 'For whom do we do it?'
3. 'How do we excel?'

In business _____, the third question is better phrased 'How can we beat or avoid competition?'. (Bradford and Duncan, page 1.)

a. 33 Strategies of War
c. 1990 Clean Air Act
b. Strategic planning
d. 28-hour day

49. _____ involves having senior executives periodically review their top executives and those in the next lower level to determine several backups for each senior position. This is important because it often takes years of grooming to develop effective senior managers. There is a critical shortage in companies of middle and top leaders for the next five years.

a. Kanban
c. Trademark
b. Risk management
d. Succession planning

50. _____ and career coaching are similar in nature to traditional counseling (Kim, Li, Lian, 2002.) However, the focus is generally on issues such as career exploration, career change, personal career development and other career related issues (Swanson, 1995.) Typically when people come for _____ they know exactly what they want to get out of the process, but are unsure about how it will work (Galassi, Crace, Martin, James, and Wallace, 1992.)

a. 33 Strategies of War
c. 1990 Clean Air Act
b. 28-hour day
d. Career counseling

51. _____ is an approach to management development where an individual is moved through a schedule of assignments designed to give him or her a breadth of exposure to the entire operation.

_____ is also practiced to allow qualified employees to gain more insights into the processes of a company, and to reduce boredom and increase job satisfaction through job variation.

The term _____ can also mean the scheduled exchange of persons in offices, especially in public offices, prior to the end of incumbency or the legislative period.

a. 1990 Clean Air Act
c. Job rotation
b. 33 Strategies of War
d. 28-hour day

52. There are two types of _____ relationships: formal and informal. Informal relationships develop on their own between partners. Formal _____, on the other hand, refers to assigned relationships, often associated with organizational _____ programs designed to promote employee development or to assist at-risk children and youth.

a. Mentoring
c. Real Property Administrator
b. Fix it twice
d. Human resource management system

Chapter 10. Human Resources Management

53. _____ is a method by which the job performance of an employee is evaluated _____ is a part of career development.

_____s are regular reviews of employee performance within organizations

Generally, the aims of a _____ are to:

- Give feedback on performance to employees.
- Identify employee training needs.
- Document criteria used to allocate organizational rewards.
- Form a basis for personnel decisions: salary increases, promotions, disciplinary actions, etc.
- Provide the opportunity for organizational diagnosis and development.
- Facilitate communication between employee and administraton
- Validate selection techniques and human resource policies to meet federal Equal Employment Opportunity requirements.

A common approach to assessing performance is to use a numerical or scalar rating system whereby managers are asked to score an individual against a number of objectives/attributes. In some companies, employees receive assessments from their manager, peers, subordinates and customers while also performing a self assessment.

a. Human resource management
b. Personnel management
c. Progressive discipline
d. Performance appraisal

54. _____ is a process of agreeing upon objectives within an organization so that management and employees agree to the objectives and understand what they are in the organization.

The term '_____' was first popularized by Peter Drucker in his 1954 book 'The Practice of Management'.

The essence of _____ is participative goal setting, choosing course of actions and decision making.

a. Management by objectives
b. Job enrichment
c. Clean sheet review
d. Business economics

55. In game theory, an _____ is a set of moves or strategies taken by the players, or their payoffs resulting from the actions or strategies taken by all players. The two are complementary in that given knowledge of the set of strategies of all players, the final state of the game is known, as are any relevant payoffs. In a game where chance or a random event is involved, the _____ is not known from only the set of strategies, but is only realized when the random event(s) are realized.
a. Outcome
b. A Stake in the Outcome
c. AAAI
d. A4e

56. _____ is a term describing performance-related pay, most frequently in the context of educational reform. It provides bonuses for workers who perform their jobs better, according to measurable criteria. In the United States, policy makers are divided on whether _____ should be offered to public school teachers, as is commonly the case in the United Kingdom.

a. Merit pay
b. Performance-related pay
c. Real wage
d. Profit-sharing agreement

57. In economics and sociology, an _____ is any factor (financial or non-financial) that enables or motivates a particular course of action, or counts as a reason for preferring one choice to the alternatives. It is an expectation that encourages people to behave in a certain way. Since human beings are purposeful creatures, the study of _____ structures is central to the study of all economic activity (both in terms of individual decision-making and in terms of co-operation and competition within a larger institutional structure.)
   a. A Stake in the Outcome
   b. A4e
   c. AAAI
   d. Incentive

58. _____ is the process of systematically determining a relative value of jobs in an organisation. In all cases the idea is to evaluate the job, not the person doing it.

   - Job Ranking is the most simple form. Basically you just order the jobs according to perceived seniority. It's easy in a small organization, but get exponentially difficult with lots of different jobs.

   - Pair Comparison introduces more rigour by comparing jobs in pairs, but really it's a more structured way of building a basic rank order.

   - Benchmarking or slotting sets up certain jobs that are analysed in detail. These are then used for comparison to slot jobs against these benchmarks.

   a. 33 Strategies of War
   b. 28-hour day
   c. 1990 Clean Air Act
   d. Job evaluation

59. The _____ of 1938 (_____, ch. 676, 52 Stat. 1060, June 25, 1938, 29 U.S.C. ch.8), also called the Wages and Hours Bill, is United States federal law that applies to employees engaged in interstate commerce or employed by an enterprise engaged in commerce or in the production of goods for commerce, unless the employer can claim an exemption from coverage. The _____ established a national minimum wage, guaranteed time and a half for overtime in certain jobs, and prohibited most employment of minors in 'oppressive child labor,' a term defined in the statute.
   a. Joint venture
   b. Board of directors
   c. Family and Medical Leave Act of 1993
   d. Fair Labor Standards Act

60. _____ are conventions, treaties and recommendations designed to eliminate unjust and inhumane labour practices. The primary inernational agency charged with developing such standards is the International Labour Organization (ILO.) Established in 1919, the ILO advocates international standards as essential for the eradication of labour conditions involving 'injustice, hardship and privation'.
   a. Anaconda Copper
   b. Airbus SAS
   c. Airbus Industrie
   d. International labour standards

Chapter 11. Managing Employee Diversity

1. The 'business case for _____', theorizes that in a global marketplace, a company that employs a diverse workforce (both men and women, people of many generations, people from ethnically and racially diverse backgrounds etc.) is better able to understand the demographics of the marketplace it serves and is thus better equipped to thrive in that marketplace than a company that has a more limited range of employee demographics.

An additional corollary suggests that a company that supports the _____ of its workforce can also improve employee satisfaction, productivity and retention.

   a. Virtual team
   b. Diversity
   c. Trademark
   d. Kanban

2.

The terms _____ and positive action refer to policies that take race, ethnicity, or gender into consideration in an attempt to promote equal opportunity. The focus of such policies ranges from employment and education to public contracting and health programs. The impetus towards _____ is twofold: to maximize diversity in all levels of society, along with its presumed benefits, and to redress perceived disadvantages due to overt, institutional, or involuntary discrimination.

   a. Adam Smith
   b. Affirmative action
   c. Abraham Harold Maslow
   d. Affiliation

3. _____ is a mathematical science pertaining to the collection, analysis, interpretation or explanation, and presentation of data. It also provides tools for prediction and forecasting based on data. It is applicable to a wide variety of academic disciplines, from the natural and social sciences to the humanities, government and business.
   a. Simple moving average
   b. Statistics
   c. Failure rate
   d. Location parameter

4. The _____ is the labour pool in employment. It is generally used to describe those working for a single company or industry, but can also apply to a geographic region like a city, country, state, etc. The term generally excludes the employers or management, and implies those involved in manual labour.
   a. Division of labour
   b. Workforce
   c. Pink-collar worker
   d. Work-life balance

5. _____ is a diversified financial services company with operations around the world. Wells Fargo is the fourth largest bank in the US by assets and the second largest bank by market cap.
   a. Committee for Economic Development
   b. Process-based management
   c. Holding company
   d. Wells Fargo ' Co.

6. _____ is an integrated communications-based process through which individuals and communities discover that existing and newly-identified needs and wants may be satisfied by the products and services of others.

_____ is defined by the American _____ Association as the activity, set of institutions, and processes for creating, communicating, delivering, and exchanging offerings that have value for customers, clients, partners, and society at large. The term developed from the original meaning which referred literally to going to market, as in shopping, or going to a market to buy or sell goods or services.

Chapter 11. Managing Employee Diversity

a. Marketing
b. Market development
c. Customer relationship management
d. Disruptive technology

7. A _____ is an entity formed between two or more parties to undertake economic activity together. The parties agree to create a new entity by both contributing equity, and they then share in the revenues, expenses, and control of the enterprise. The venture can be for one specific project only, or a continuing business relationship such as the Fuji Xerox _____.
   a. Civil Rights Act of 1991
   b. Patent
   c. Meritor Savings Bank v. Vinson
   d. Joint venture

8. An _____ is a person who has possession of an enterprise and assumes significant accountability for the inherent risks and the outcome. It is an ambitious leader who combines land, labor, and capital to create and market new goods or services. The term is a loanword from French and was first defined by the Irish economist Richard Cantillon.
   a. AAAI
   b. A4e
   c. A Stake in the Outcome
   d. Entrepreneur

9. In economics, the term _____ refers to situations where the advancement of a qualified person within the hierarchy of an organization is stopped at a lower level because of some form of discrimination, most commonly sexism or racism, but since the term was coined, '_____' has also come to describe the limited advancement of the deaf, blind, disabled, aged and sexual minorities. It is an unofficial, invisible barrier that prevents women and minorities from advancing in businesses.

This situation is referred to as a 'ceiling' as there is a limitation blocking upward advancement, and 'glass' (transparent) because the limitation is not immediately apparent and is normally an unwritten and unofficial policy. This invisible barrier continues to exist, even though there are no explicit obstacles keeping minorities from acquiring advanced job positions - there are no advertisements that specifically say 'no minorities hired at this establishment', nor are there any formal orders that say 'minorities are not qualified' - but they do lie beneath the surface.

   a. 28-hour day
   b. 1990 Clean Air Act
   c. 33 Strategies of War
   d. Glass ceiling

10. _____ is a type of thought exhibited by group members who try to minimize conflict and reach consensus without critically testing, analyzing, and evaluating ideas. Individual creativity, uniqueness, and independent thinking are lost in the pursuit of group cohesiveness, as are the advantages of reasonable balance in choice and thought that might normally be obtained by making decisions as a group. During _____, members of the group avoid promoting viewpoints outside the comfort zone of consensus thinking.
    a. Self-report inventory
    b. Diffusion of responsibility
    c. Psychological statistics
    d. Groupthink

11. _____ is a subfield of the larger discipline of communication studies. _____, as a field, is the consideration, analysis, and criticism of the role of communication in organizational contexts.

The field traces its lineage through business information, business communication, and early mass communication studies published in the 1930s through the 1950s.

Chapter 11. Managing Employee Diversity

a. A4e
b. A Stake in the Outcome
c. Organizational communication
d. AAAI

12. _____ can be regarded as an outcome of mental processes (cognitive process) leading to the selection of a course of action among several alternatives. Every _____ process produces a final choice. The output can be an action or an opinion of choice.
a. 28-hour day
b. 33 Strategies of War
c. Decision making
d. 1990 Clean Air Act

13. _____ is a contract between two parties, one being the employer and the other being the employee. An employee may be defined as: 'A person in the service of another under any contract of hire, express or implied, oral or written, where the employer has the power or right to control and direct the employee in the material details of how the work is to be performed.' Black's Law Dictionary page 471 (5th ed. 1979.)
a. Exit interview
b. Employment
c. Employment counsellor
d. Employment rate

14. The term _____ was created by President Lyndon B. Johnson when he signed Executive Order 11246 on September 24, 1965, created to prohibit federal contractors from discriminating against employees on the basis of race, sex, creed, religion, color, or national origin. In more recent times, most employers have also added sexual orientation to the list of non-discrimination.

The Executive Order also required contractors to implement affirmative action plans to increase the participation of minorities and women in the workplace.

a. A Stake in the Outcome
b. Equal Employment Opportunity
c. AAAI
d. A4e

15. The U.S. _____ is a federal agency whose goal is ending employment discrimination. The _____ investigates discrimination complaints based on an individual's race, color, national origin, religion, sex, age, disability and retaliation for reporting and/or opposing a discriminatory practice. The Commission is also tasked with filing suits on behalf of alleged victim(s) of discrimination against employers and as an adjudicatory for claims of discrimination brought against federal agencies.
a. ARCO
b. Airbus Industrie
c. Equal Employment Opportunity Commission
d. Airbus SAS

16. _____ is the strategic and coherent approach to the management of an organisation's most valued assets - the people working there who individually and collectively contribute to the achievement of the objectives of the business. The terms '_____' and 'human resources' (HR) have largely replaced the term 'personnel management' as a description of the processes involved in managing people in organizations. In simple sense, _____ means employing people, developing their resources, utilizing, maintaining and compensating their services in tune with the job and organizational requirement.
a. Job knowledge
b. Progressive discipline
c. Human resource management
d. Revolving door syndrome

17. _____ is a term defined by the Oxford English Dictionary as an individual's 'course or progress through life '. It is usually considered to pertain to remunerative work (and sometimes also formal education.)

The etymology of the term is somewhat ironic in that it comes from the Latin word carrera, which means race .

a. Career planning
b. Spatial mismatch
c. Career
d. Nursing shortage

18. In organizational development (or OD), the study of _____ looks at:

- how individuals manage their careers within and between organizations
- and how organizations structure the career progress of their members, it can also be tied into succession planning within some organizations.

In personal development, _____ is:

- ' ... the total constellation of psychological, sociological, educational, physical, economic, and chance factors that combine to influence the nature and significance of work in the total lifespan of any given individual.'

- '... the lifelong psychological and behavioral processes as well as contextual influences shaping one's career over the life span. As such, _____ involves the person's creation of a career pattern, decision-making style, integration of life roles, values expression, and life-role self concepts.'

Figures in _____

- Jeff A. Brown
- Jesse B. Davis
- Caela Farren
- John L. Holland
- Kris Magnusson
- Frank Parsons
- Vance Peavy
- Edgar Schein
- Rino Schreuder
- Mark L. Savickas
- Donald Super

a. Sole proprietorship
b. Horizontal integration
c. Business process reengineering
d. Career development

Chapter 11. Managing Employee Diversity

19. _____ is a process of planning and controlling the performance or execution of any type of activity, such as:

- a project (project _____) or
- a process (process _____, sometimes referred to as the process performance measurement and management system.)

Organization's senior management is responsible for carrying out its _____.

a. Participatory management
c. Work design
b. Human Relations Movement
d. Management process

20. In law, _____ is the term to describe a partnership between two or more parties.

In England a number of statutes on the subject have been passed, the chief being the Bastardy Act of 1845, and the Bastardy Laws Amendment Acts of 1872 and 1873. The mother of a bastard may summon the putative father to petty sessions within twelve months of the birth (or at any later time if he is proved to have contributed to the child's support within twelve months after the birth), and the justices, as after hearing evidence on both sides, may, if the mother's evidence be corroborated in some material particular, adjudge the man to be the putative father of the child, and order him to pay a sum not exceeding five shillings a week for its maintenance, together with a sum for expenses incidental to the birth, or the funeral expenses, if it has died before the date of order, and the costs of the proceedings.

a. Affiliation
c. Abraham Harold Maslow
b. Affiliation
d. Adam Smith

21. _____ is a method by which the job performance of an employee is evaluated _____ is a part of career development.

_____s are regular reviews of employee performance within organizations

Generally, the aims of a _____ are to:

- Give feedback on performance to employees.
- Identify employee training needs.
- Document criteria used to allocate organizational rewards.
- Form a basis for personnel decisions: salary increases, promotions, disciplinary actions, etc.
- Provide the opportunity for organizational diagnosis and development.
- Facilitate communication between employee and administraton
- Validate selection techniques and human resource policies to meet federal Equal Employment Opportunity requirements.

A common approach to assessing performance is to use a numerical or scalar rating system whereby managers are asked to score an individual against a number of objectives/attributes. In some companies, employees receive assessments from their manager, peers, subordinates and customers while also performing a self assessment.

a. Progressive discipline
b. Personnel management
c. Human resource management
d. Performance appraisal

22. _____ is a broad concept including proper prioritizing between career and ambition on one hand, compared with pleasure, leisure, family and spiritual development on the other.

As the separation between work and home life has diminished, this concept has become more relevant than ever before.

The expression was first used in the late 1970s to describe the balance between an individual's work and personal life.

a. Division of labour
b. Workforce
c. Quality of working life
d. Work-life balance

23. _____ is unwelcome harassment of a sexual nature, or based upon the receiving party's sex or gender. In some contexts or circumstances, _____ may be illegal. It includes a range of behavior from seemingly mild transgressions and annoyances to actual sexual abuse or sexual assault.

a. 28-hour day
b. 1990 Clean Air Act
c. Sexual harassment
d. Hypernorms

24. _____ is a concept in ethics with several meanings. It is often used synonymously with such concepts as responsibility, answerability, enforcement, blameworthiness, liability and other terms associated with the expectation of account-giving. As an aspect of governance, it has been central to discussions related to problems in both the public and private (corporation) worlds.

a. A Stake in the Outcome
b. A4e
c. Usury
d. Accountability

25. The general definition of an _____ is an evaluation of a person, organization, system, process, project or product. _____s are performed to ascertain the validity and reliability of information; also to provide an assessment of a system's internal control. The goal of an _____ is to express an opinion on the person / organization/system (etc) in question, under evaluation based on work done on a test basis.

a. A Stake in the Outcome
b. Audit
c. Audit committee
d. Internal control

26. _____ is a system of training a new generation of practitioners of a skill. Apprentices (or in early modern usage 'prentices') or prot>ég>és build their careers from _____s. Most of their training is done on the job while working for an employer who helps the apprentices learn their trade, in exchange for their continuing labour for an agreed period after they become skilled.

a. A Stake in the Outcome
b. A4e
c. AAAI
d. Apprenticeship

27. _____ is training for the purpose of increasing participants' cultural awareness, knowledge, and skills, which is based on the assumption that the training will benefit an organization by protecting against civil rights violations, increasing the inclusion of different identity groups, and promoting better teamwork.

Chapter 11. Managing Employee Diversity

_____ has been a controversial issue, due to moral considerations as well as questioned efficiency or even counterproductivity.

According to Michael Bird, many project managers may feel that they are treading new territory as they lead project teams made of individuals from different cultures, heterogeneous mixes, and differing demographics.

a. Diversity training
c. Self-disclosure
b. Soft skill
d. Role conflict

28. There are two types of _____ relationships: formal and informal. Informal relationships develop on their own between partners. Formal _____, on the other hand, refers to assigned relationships, often associated with organizational _____ programs designed to promote employee development or to assist at-risk children and youth.

a. Fix it twice
c. Human resource management system
b. Mentoring
d. Real Property Administrator

29. Procter is a surname, and may also refer to:

- Bryan Waller Procter (pseud. Barry Cornwall), English poet
- Goodwin Procter, American law firm
- _____, consumer products multinational

a. Downstream
c. Procter ' Gamble
b. Strict liability
d. Master and Servant Acts

30. The term '_____' refers to the concept of collecting information and attempting to spot a pattern in the information. In some fields of study, the term '_____' has more formally-defined meanings.

In project management _____ is a mathematical technique that uses historical results to predict future outcome.

a. Least squares
c. Stepwise regression
b. Regression analysis
d. Trend analysis

Chapter 12. Motivation

1. Clayton Paul Alderfer is an American psychologist who further expanded Maslow's hierarchy of needs by categorizing the hierarchy into his _____ Alderfer categorized the lower order needs (Physiological and Safety) into the Existence category. He fit Maslow's interpersonal love and esteem needs into the relatedness category. The growth category contained the Self Actualization and self esteem needs.

   Alderfer also proposed a regression theory to go along with the _____. He said that when needs in a higher category are not met then individuals redouble the efforts invested in a lower category need.

   a. Adam Smith
   b. Abraham Harold Maslow
   c. Alvin Neill Jackson
   d. ERG theory

2. _____ comes from outside of the performer. Money is the most obvious example, but coercion and threat of punishment are also common _____ s.

   In sports, the crowd may cheer the performer on, and this motivates him or her to do well.

   a. A4e
   b. A Stake in the Outcome
   c. Intrinsic motivation
   d. Extrinsic motivation

3. _____ comes from rewards inherent to a task or activity itself - the enjoyment of a puzzle or the love of playing basketball, for example. One is said to be intrinsically motivated when engaging in an activity 'with no apparent reward except for the activity itself'. This form of motivation has been studied by social and educational psychologists since the early 1970s.

   a. Extrinsic motivation
   b. Intrinsic motivation
   c. A4e
   d. A Stake in the Outcome

4. _____ was developed by Frederick Herzberg, a psychologist who found that job satisfaction and job dissatisfaction acted independently of each other. _____ states that there are certain factors in the workplace that cause job satisfaction, while a separate set of factors cause dissatisfaction.

   a. 1990 Clean Air Act
   b. Two-factor theory
   c. Need for power
   d. Need for Achievement

5. Maslow's _____ is a theory in psychology, proposed by Abraham Maslow in his 1943 paper A Theory of Human Motivation, which he subsequently extended to include his observations of humans' innate curiosity.

   Maslow's _____ is predetermined in order of importance. It is often depicted as a pyramid consisting of five levels: the lowest level is associated with physiological needs, while the uppermost level is associated with self-actualization needs, particularly those related to identity and purpose. Deficiency needs must be met first. Once these are met, seeking to satisfy growth needs drives personal growth. The higher needs in this hierarchy only come into focus when the lower needs in the pyramid are met.

   a. 33 Strategies of War
   b. 28-hour day
   c. Hierarchy of needs
   d. 1990 Clean Air Act

6. _____ is a term that has been used in various psychology theories, often in slightly different ways (e.g., Goldstein, Maslow, Rogers.) The term was originally introduced by the organismic theorist Kurt Goldstein for the motive to realise all of one's potentialities. In his view, it is the master motive--indeed, the only real motive a person has, all others being merely manifestations of it.

Chapter 12. Motivation

a. 28-hour day
c. 33 Strategies of War
b. 1990 Clean Air Act
d. Self-actualization

7. In law, _____ is the term to describe a partnership between two or more parties.

In England a number of statutes on the subject have been passed, the chief being the Bastardy Act of 1845, and the Bastardy Laws Amendment Acts of 1872 and 1873. The mother of a bastard may summon the putative father to petty sessions within twelve months of the birth (or at any later time if he is proved to have contributed to the child's support within twelve months after the birth), and the justices, as after hearing evidence on both sides, may, if the mother's evidence be corroborated in some material particular, adjudge the man to be the putative father of the child, and order him to pay a sum not exceeding five shillings a week for its maintenance, together with a sum for expenses incidental to the birth, or the funeral expenses, if it has died before the date of order, and the costs of the proceedings.

a. Abraham Harold Maslow
c. Affirmative action
b. Adam Smith
d. Affiliation

8. _____ has become one of the most popular theories in organizational psychology.

Goal setting has been a formula used for acheivement since the early 1800s. The form and pattern has cahanged drastically over the years and there is still much debate as to what is the most efective pattern to follow.

a. Goal-setting theory
c. Job satisfaction
b. Corporate Culture
d. Human relations

9. _____ is a process of agreeing upon objectives within an organization so that management and employees agree to the objectives and understand what they are in the organization.

The term '_____' was first popularized by Peter Drucker in his 1954 book 'The Practice of Management'.

The essence of _____ is participative goal setting, choosing course of actions and decision making.

a. Clean sheet review
c. Job enrichment
b. Business economics
d. Management by objectives

10. _____ attempts to explain relational satisfaction in terms of perceptions of fair/unfair distributions of resources within interpersonal relationships. _____ is considered as one of the justice theories, It was first developed in 1962 by John Stacey Adams, a workplace and behavioral psychologist, who asserted that employees seek to maintain equity between the inputs that they bring to a job and the outcomes that they receive from it against the perceived inputs and outcomes of others (Adams, 1965.) The belief is that people value fair treatment which causes them to be motivated to keep the fairness maintained within the relationships of their co-workers and the organization.

a. A Stake in the Outcome
c. AAAI
b. A4e
d. Equity theory

Chapter 12. Motivation

11. In operant conditioning, _____ occurs when an event following a response causes an increase in the probability of that response occurring in the future. Response strength can be assessed by measures such as the frequency with which the response is made (for example, a pigeon may peck a key more times in the session), or the speed with which it is made (for example, a rat may run a maze faster.) The environment change contingent upon the response is called a reinforcer.

   a. Meetings, Incentives, Conferences, and Exhibitions
   b. Historiometry
   c. Diminishing Manufacturing Sources and Material Shortages
   d. Reinforcement

12. An _____ is a person who has possession of an enterprise and assumes significant accountability for the inherent risks and the outcome. It is an ambitious leader who combines land, labor, and capital to create and market new goods or services. The term is a loanword from French and was first defined by the Irish economist Richard Cantillon.

   a. A Stake in the Outcome
   b. AAAI
   c. A4e
   d. Entrepreneur

13. _____ is a term defined by the Oxford English Dictionary as an individual's 'course or progress through life '. It is usually considered to pertain to remunerative work (and sometimes also formal education.)

   The etymology of the term is somewhat ironic in that it comes from the Latin word carrera, which means race .

   a. Spatial mismatch
   b. Career
   c. Career planning
   d. Nursing shortage

14. _____ is about the mental processes regarding choice, or choosing. It explains the processes that an individual undergoes to make choices. In organizational behavior study, _____ is a motivation theory first proposed by Victor Vroom of the Yale School of Management.

   a. AAAI
   b. Expectancy theory
   c. A Stake in the Outcome
   d. A4e

15. In organizational development (OD), _____ is the application of Socio-Technical Systems principles and techniques to the humanization of work.

   The aims of _____ to improved job satisfaction, to improved through-put, to improved quality and to reduced employee problems, e.g., grievances, absenteeism.

   Under scientific management people would be directed by reason and the problems of industrial unrest would be appropriately (i.e., scientifically) addressed.

   a. Path-goal theory
   b. Graduate recruitment
   c. Work design
   d. Management process

16. _____ means increasing the scope of a job through extending the range of its job duties and responsibilities. This contradicts the principles of specialisation and the division of labour whereby work is divided into small units, each of which is performed repetitively by an individual worker. Some motivational theories suggest that the boredom and alienation caused by the division of labour can actually cause efficiency to fall.

Chapter 12. Motivation

a. Centralization
b. Mock interview
c. Job enlargement
d. Delayering

17. _____ is an attempt to motivate employees by giving them the opportunity to use the range of their abilities. It is an idea that was developed by the American psychologist Frederick Herzberg in the 1950s. It can be contrasted to job enlargement which simply increases the number of tasks without changing the challenge.

a. Catfish effect
b. Job enrichment
c. Cash cow
d. C-A-K-E

18. _____ is an approach to management development where an individual is moved through a schedule of assignments designed to give him or her a breadth of exposure to the entire operation.

_____ is also practiced to allow qualified employees to gain more insights into the processes of a company, and to reduce boredom and increase job satisfaction through job variation.

The term _____ can also mean the scheduled exchange of persons in offices, especially in public offices, prior to the end of incumbency or the legislative period.

a. Job rotation
b. 28-hour day
c. 1990 Clean Air Act
d. 33 Strategies of War

19. _____ refers to increasing the spiritual, political, social or economic strength of individuals and communities. It often involves the empowered developing confidence in their own capacities.

The term Human _____ covers a vast landscape of meanings, interpretations, definitions and disciplines ranging from psychology and philosophy to the highly commercialized Self-Help industry and Motivational sciences.

a. A4e
b. AAAI
c. Empowerment
d. A Stake in the Outcome

20. _____ has been described as the 'process of social influence in which one person can enlist the aid and support of others in the accomplishment of a common task' . A definition more inclusive of followers comes from Alan Keith of Genentech who said '_____ is ultimately about creating a way for people to contribute to making something extraordinary happen.'

_____ is one of the most salient aspects of the organizational context. However, defining _____ has been challenging.

a. 28-hour day
b. Situational leadership
c. 1990 Clean Air Act
d. Leadership

21. _____ involves establishing specific, measurable and time-targeted objectives. Work on the theory of goal-setting suggests that it's an effective tool for making progress by ensuring that participants in a group with a common goal are clearly aware of what is expected from them if an objective is to be achieved. On a personal level, setting goals is a process that allows people to specify then work towards their own objectives - most commonly with financial or career-based goals.

a. Catfish effect
b. Digital strategy
c. Resource-based view
d. Goal setting

Chapter 13. Leadership

1. _____ has been described as the 'process of social influence in which one person can enlist the aid and support of others in the accomplishment of a common task'. A definition more inclusive of followers comes from Alan Keith of Genentech who said '_____ is ultimately about creating a way for people to contribute to making something extraordinary happen.'

_____ is one of the most salient aspects of the organizational context. However, defining _____ has been challenging.

a. Situational leadership
b. 1990 Clean Air Act
c. 28-hour day
d. Leadership

2. A _____ is a name or trademark connected with a product or producer. _____s have become increasingly important components of culture and the economy, now being described as 'cultural accessories and personal philosophies'.

Some people distinguish the psychological aspect of a _____ from the experiential aspect.

a. Brand loyalty
b. Brand
c. Brand extension
d. Brand awareness

3. _____ is individual power based on a high level of identification with, admiration of, or respect for the powerholder.

Nationalism, Patriotism, Celebrities and well-respected people are examples of _____ in effect.

_____ is one of the Five Bases of Social Power, as defined by Bertram Raven and his colleagues[1] in 1959.

a. Referent power
b. 28-hour day
c. 33 Strategies of War
d. 1990 Clean Air Act

4. In psychology, _____ is a major approach to the study of human personality. Trait theorists are primarily interested in the measurement of traits, which can be defined as habitual patterns of behavior, thought, and emotion. According to this perspective, traits are relatively stable over time, differ among individuals (e.g. some people are outgoing whereas others are shy), and influence behavior.

a. Psychometrics
b. Psychological statistics
c. Trait theory
d. Cognitive dissonance

5. _____ is a form of applied ethics that examines ethical principles and moral or ethical problems that arise in a business environment. It applies to all aspects of business conduct and is relevant to the conduct of individuals and business organizations as a whole. Applied ethics is a field of ethics that deals with ethical questions in many fields such as medical, technical, legal and _____.

a. Business ethics
b. Hypernorms
c. Facilitation payments
d. Corporate Sustainability

6. _____ is a term used to describe a policy of allowing events to take their own course. The term is a French phrase literally meaning 'let do'. It is a doctrine that states that government generally should not intervene in the marketplace.

Chapter 13. Leadership

a. Laissez-faire
b. Deep ecology
c. Freedom of contract
d. Libertarian

7. Contingency leadership theory in organizational studies is a type of leadership theory, leadership style, and leadership model that presumes that different leadership styles are contingent to different situations. It is also referred as _____ Â® theory although, as originally convened, the situational theory term is much more restrictive. The original situational theory argues that the best type of leadership is totally determined by the situational variables.Currently there are many styles of leadership.

a. 28-hour day
b. Situational theory
c. Situational Leadership
d. 1990 Clean Air Act

8. The _____ is a leadership theory in the field of organizational studies developed by Robert House in 1971 and revised in 1996. The theory that a leader's behavior is contingent to the satisfaction, motivation and performance of subordinates. The revised version also argues that the leader engage in behaviors that complement subordinate's abilities and compensate for deficiencies.

a. Corporate Culture
b. Sociotechnical systems
c. Path-goal theory
d. Human relations

9. _____ refers to increasing the spiritual, political, social or economic strength of individuals and communities. It often involves the empowered developing confidence in their own capacities.

The term Human _____ covers a vast landscape of meanings, interpretations, definitions and disciplines ranging from psychology and philosophy to the highly commercialized Self-Help industry and Motivational sciences.

a. AAAI
b. A4e
c. A Stake in the Outcome
d. Empowerment

10. _____ is a term used to classify a group leadership theories that inquire the interactions between leaders and followers. A transactional leader focuses more on a series of 'transactions'. This person is interested in looking out for oneself, having exchange benefits with their subordinates and clarify a sense of duty with rewards and punishments to reach goals.

a. 28-hour day
b. Transactional leadership
c. 1990 Clean Air Act
d. 33 Strategies of War

11. _____ of the learning curve effect and the closely related experience curve effect express the relationship between equations for experience and efficiency or between efficiency gains and investment in the effort. The experience of 'learning curves' was first observed by the 19th Century German psychologist Hermann Ebbinghaus according to the difficulty of memorizing varying numbers of verbal stimuli, and subsequent learning about the complex processes of learning are discussed in the

.

The rule used for representing the learning curve effect states that the more times a task has been performed, the less time will be required on each subsequent iteration.

a. Distribution
b. Spatial Decision Support Systems
c. Point biserial correlation coefficient
d. Models

12. _____ is a leadership style that defines as leadership that creates voluble and positive change in the followers. A transformational leader focuses on 'transforming' others to help each other, to look out for each other, be encouraging, harmonious, and look out for the organization as a whole. In this leadership, the leader enhances the motivation, moral and performance of his follower group.
a. SESAMO
b. Polynomial conjoint measurement
c. Strong-Campbell Interest Inventory
d. Transformational leadership

Chapter 14. Managing Teams

1. _____ is the term used to describe a situation where different entities cooperate advantageously for a final outcome. Simply defined, it means that the whole is greater than the sum of the individual parts. Although the whole will be greater than each individual part, this is not the concept of _____.
   - a. 28-hour day
   - b. 33 Strategies of War
   - c. 1990 Clean Air Act
   - d. Synergy

2. _____ refers to metrics and measures of output from production processes, per unit of input. Labor _____, for example, is typically measured as a ratio of output per labor-hour, an input. _____ may be conceived of as a metrics of the technical or engineering efficiency of production.
   - a. Value engineering
   - b. Productivity
   - c. Master production schedule
   - d. Remanufacturing

3. In economics, business, retail, and accounting, a _____ is the value of money that has been used up to produce something, and hence is not available for use anymore. In economics, a _____ is an alternative that is given up as a result of a decision. In business, the _____ may be one of acquisition, in which case the amount of money expended to acquire it is counted as _____.
   - a. Cost allocation
   - b. Cost
   - c. Fixed costs
   - d. Cost overrun

4. A _____ or business method is a collection of related, structured activities or tasks that produce a specific service or product (serve a particular goal) for a particular customer or customers. It often can be visualized with a flowchart as a sequence of activities.

   There are three types of _____es:

   1. Management processes, the processes that govern the operation of a system. Typical management processes include 'Corporate Governance' and 'Strategic Management'.
   2. Operational processes, processes that constitute the core business and create the primary value stream. Typical operational processes are Purchasing, Manufacturing, Marketing, and Sales.
   3. Supporting processes, which support the core processes. Examples include Accounting, Recruitment, Technical support.

   A _____ begins with a customer's need and ends with a customer's need fulfillment. Process oriented organizations break down the barriers of structural departments and try to avoid functional silos.

   - a. Business process
   - b. 33 Strategies of War
   - c. 1990 Clean Air Act
   - d. 28-hour day

5. _____ is, in very basic words, a position a firm occupies against its competitors.

According to Michael Porter, the three methods for creating a sustainable _____ are through:

1. Cost leadership

2. Differentiation

Chapter 14. Managing Teams

3. Focus (economics)

 a. Theory Z
 c. 28-hour day
 b. Competitive advantage
 d. 1990 Clean Air Act

6. The 'business case for _____', theorizes that in a global marketplace, a company that employs a diverse workforce (both men and women, people of many generations, people from ethnically and racially diverse backgrounds etc.) is better able to understand the demographics of the marketplace it serves and is thus better equipped to thrive in that marketplace than a company that has a more limited range of employee demographics.

An additional corollary suggests that a company that supports the _____ of its workforce can also improve employee satisfaction, productivity and retention.

 a. Kanban
 c. Trademark
 b. Diversity
 d. Virtual team

7. _____ refers to the movement of cash into or out of a business or financial product. It is usually measured during a specified, finite period of time. Measurement of _____ can be used

- to determine a project's rate of return or value. The time of _____s into and out of projects are used as inputs in financial models such as internal rate of return, and net present value.
- to determine problems with a business's liquidity. Being profitable does not necessarily mean being liquid. A company can fail because of a shortage of cash, even while profitable.
- as an alternate measure of a business's profits when it is believed that accrual accounting concepts do not represent economic realities. For example, a company may be notionally profitable but generating little operational cash (as may be the case for a company that barters its products rather than selling for cash.) In such a case, the company may be deriving additional operating cash by issuing shares evaluating default risk, re-investment requirements, etc.

_____ is a generic term used differently depending on the context. It may be defined by users for their own purposes.

 a. Sweat equity
 c. Gross profit
 b. Gross profit margin
 d. Cash flow

8. A _____ -- also known as a geographically dispersed team -- is a group of individuals who work across time, space, and organizational boundaries with links strengthened by webs of communication technology. They have complementary skills and are committed to a common purpose, have interdependent performance goals, and share an approach to work for which they hold themselves mutually accountable. Geographically dispersed teams allow organizations to hire and retain the best people regardless of location.

 a. Virtual team
 c. Trademark
 b. Kanban
 d. Risk management

9. The _____ (Situation, Task, Action, Result) format is a job interview technique used by interviewers to gather all the relevant information about a specific capability that the job requires. This interview format is said to have a higher degree of predictability of future on-the-job performance than the traditional interview.

- Situation: The interviewer wants you to present a recent challenge and situation in which you found yourself.
- Task: What did you have to achieve? The interviewer will be looking to see what you were trying to achieve from the situation.
- Action: What did you do? The interviewer will be looking for information on what you did, why you did it and what were the alternatives.
- Results: What was the outcome of your actions? What did you achieve through your actions and did you meet your objectives. What did you learn from this experience and have you used this learning since?

a. Star
b. Phrase completion
c. Rasch models
d. Competency-based job descriptions

10. _____ is a civil designation for persons who are incorporated in a fixed or permanent way to a society or group: regular member of the working staff, permanent staff distinguished from a supernumerary.

The term '_____' and its counterpart, 'supernumerary,' originated in Spanish and Latin American academy and government; it is now also used in countries all over the world, such as France, the U.S., England, Italy, etc.

There are _____ members of surgical organizations, of universities, of gastronomical associations, etc.

a. Abraham Harold Maslow
b. Adam Smith
c. Affiliation
d. Numerary

11. _____ has been described as the 'process of social influence in which one person can enlist the aid and support of others in the accomplishment of a common task'. A definition more inclusive of followers comes from Alan Keith of Genentech who said '_____ is ultimately about creating a way for people to contribute to making something extraordinary happen.'

_____ is one of the most salient aspects of the organizational context. However, defining _____ has been challenging.

a. 28-hour day
b. 1990 Clean Air Act
c. Situational leadership
d. Leadership

12. _____ is a dynamic of being mutually and physically responsible to and sharing a common set of principles with others. This concept differs distinctly from 'dependence' in that an interdependent relationship implies that all participants are emotionally, economically, ecologically and or morally 'interdependent.' Some people advocate freedom or independence as a sort of ultimate good; others do the same with devotion to one's family, community, or society. _____ recognizes the truth in each position and weaves them together.

a. AAAI
b. A Stake in the Outcome
c. A4e
d. Interdependence

Chapter 14. Managing Teams

13. _____ refers to the long-term management of intractable conflicts. It is the label for the variety of ways by which people handle grievances--standing up for what they consider to be right and against what they consider to be wrong. Those ways include such diverse phenomena as gossip, ridicule, lynching, terrorism, warfare, feuding, genocide, law, mediation, and avoidance.
   a. 33 Strategies of War
   b. 28-hour day
   c. 1990 Clean Air Act
   d. Conflict management

14. _____ can be regarded as an outcome of mental processes (cognitive process) leading to the selection of a course of action among several alternatives. Every _____ process produces a final choice. The output can be an action or an opinion of choice.
   a. 1990 Clean Air Act
   b. 33 Strategies of War
   c. 28-hour day
   d. Decision making

15. _____ is an interdisciplinary field of science and the study of the nature of complex systems in nature, society, and science. More specifically, it is a framework by which one can analyze and/or describe any group of objects that work in concert to produce some result. This could be a single organism, any organization or society, or any electro-mechanical or informational artifact.
   a. 28-hour day
   b. 1990 Clean Air Act
   c. Systems thinking
   d. Systems theory

Chapter 15. Managing Communication

1. A _____ in today's workforce is an individual that is valued for their ability to interpret information within a specific subject area. They will often advance the overall understanding of that subject through focused analysis, design and/or development. They use research skills to define problems and to identify alternatives.

   a. Business rule
   b. Customer satisfaction
   c. Career development
   d. Knowledge worker

2. _____ is a subfield of the larger discipline of communication studies. _____, as a field, is the consideration, analysis, and criticism of the role of communication in organizational contexts.

   The field traces its lineage through business information, business communication, and early mass communication studies published in the 1930s through the 1950s.

   a. A4e
   b. A Stake in the Outcome
   c. Organizational communication
   d. AAAI

3. _____ is the systematic planning, implementing, monitoring, and revision of all the channels of communication within an organization, and between organizations; it also includes the organization and dissemination of new communication directives connected with an organization, network, or communications technology. Aspects of _____ include developing corporate communication strategies, designing internal and external communications directives, and managing the flow of information, including online communication. New technology forces constant innovation on the part of communications managers.

   a. Adam Smith
   b. Abraham Harold Maslow
   c. Affiliation
   d. Communications Management

4. _____ describes the situation when output from (or information about the result of) an event or phenomenon in the past will influence the same event/phenomenon in the present or future. When an event is part of a chain of cause-and-effect that forms a circuit or loop, then the event is said to 'feed back' into itself.

   _____ is also a synonym for:

   - _____ signal; the information about the initial event that is the basis for subsequent modification of the event.
   - _____ loop; the causal path that leads from the initial generation of the _____ signal to the subsequent modification of the event.

   _____ is a mechanism, process or signal that is looped back to control a system within itself. Such a loop is called a _____ loop.

   a. 1990 Clean Air Act
   b. Feedback
   c. Positive feedback
   d. Feedback loop

5. _____ in Public Relations

   There are different types of _____ in public relations; symmetric and asymmetric.

Chapter 15. Managing Communication

Two-way asymmetric public relations...>· can also be called 'scientific persuasion;'>· employs social science methods to develop more persuasive communication;>· generally focuses on achieving short-term attitude change;>· incorporates lots of feedback from target audiences and publics;>· is used by an organization primarily interested in having its publics come around to its way of thinking rather changing the organization, its policies, or its views.

Two-way symmetric public relations...>· relies on honest and open _____ and mutual give-and-take rather than one-way persuasion;>· focuses on mutual respect and efforts to achieve mutual understanding;>· emphasizes negotiation and a willingness to adapt and make compromises;>· requires organizations engaging in public relations to be willing to make significant adjustments in how they operate in order to accommodate their publics;>· seems to be used more by non-profit organizations, government agencies, and heavily regulated businesses such as public utilities than by competitive, profit-driven companies.

- a. 28-hour day
- b. Two-way communication
- c. Public relations
- d. 1990 Clean Air Act

6. _____ is an international professional services company, whose main expertise is consultancy-based coaching and training. _____ is headquartered in Brussels, Belgium and has 25 offices in 16 countries.

_____ International was founded by Eric _____ in 1971 in Switzerland.

- a. Personal trainer
- b. National Occupational Standards
- c. Karuna Institute
- d. Krauthammer

7. A _____ -- also known as a geographically dispersed team -- is a group of individuals who work across time, space, and organizational boundaries with links strengthened by webs of communication technology. They have complementary skills and are committed to a common purpose, have interdependent performance goals, and share an approach to work for which they hold themselves mutually accountable. Geographically dispersed teams allow organizations to hire and retain the best people regardless of location.
- a. Risk management
- b. Virtual team
- c. Kanban
- d. Trademark

8. _____ is a form of applied ethics that examines ethical principles and moral or ethical problems that arise in a business environment. It applies to all aspects of business conduct and is relevant to the conduct of individuals and business organizations as a whole. Applied ethics is a field of ethics that deals with ethical questions in many fields such as medical, technical, legal and _____.
- a. Hypernorms
- b. Business ethics
- c. Corporate Sustainability
- d. Facilitation payments

9. _____ is an idea in the field of Organizational studies and management which describes the psychology, attitudes, experiences, beliefs and Values (personal and cultural values) of an organization. It has been defined as 'the specific collection of values and norms that are shared by people and groups in an organization and that control the way they interact with each other and with stakeholders outside the organization.'

This definition continues to explain organizational values also known as 'beliefs and ideas about what kinds of goals members of an organization should pursue and ideas about the appropriate kinds or standards of behavior organizational members should use to achieve these goals. From organizational values develop organizational norms, guidelines or expectations that prescribe appropriate kinds of behavior by employees in particular situations and control the behavior of organizational members towards one another.'

_____ is not the same as corporate culture.

a. Organizational development
b. Organizational effectiveness
c. Union shop
d. Organizational culture

10. The 'business case for _____', theorizes that in a global marketplace, a company that employs a diverse workforce (both men and women, people of many generations, people from ethnically and racially diverse backgrounds etc.) is better able to understand the demographics of the marketplace it serves and is thus better equipped to thrive in that marketplace than a company that has a more limited range of employee demographics.

An additional corollary suggests that a company that supports the _____ of its workforce can also improve employee satisfaction, productivity and retention.

a. Kanban
b. Trademark
c. Diversity
d. Virtual team

Chapter 16. Management Control

1. _____ is one of the managerial functions like planning, organizing, staffing and directing. It is an important function because it helps to check the errors and to take the corrective action so that deviation from standards are minimized and stated goals of the organization are achieved in desired manner. According to modern concepts, _____ is a foreseeing action whereas earlier concept of _____ was used only when errors were detected. _____ in management means setting standards, measuring actual performance and taking corrective action.

   a. Schedule of reinforcement
   b. Turnover
   c. Control
   d. Decision tree pruning

2. The _____ is a performance management tool for measuring whether the smaller-scale operational activities of a company are aligned with its larger-scale objectives in terms of vision and strategy.

   By focusing not only on financial outcomes but also on the operational, marketing and developmental inputs to these, the _____ helps provide a more comprehensive view of a business, which in turn helps organizations act in their best long-term interests. This tool is also being used to address business response to climate change and greenhouse gas emissions.

   a. Balanced scorecard
   b. Commercial management
   c. Middle management
   d. Management development

3. _____ is a form of applied ethics that examines ethical principles and moral or ethical problems that arise in a business environment. It applies to all aspects of business conduct and is relevant to the conduct of individuals and business organizations as a whole. Applied ethics is a field of ethics that deals with ethical questions in many fields such as medical, technical, legal and _____.

   a. Hypernorms
   b. Corporate Sustainability
   c. Facilitation payments
   d. Business ethics

4. _____ describes the situation when output from (or information about the result of) an event or phenomenon in the past will influence the same event/phenomenon in the present or future. When an event is part of a chain of cause-and-effect that forms a circuit or loop, then the event is said to 'feed back' into itself.

   _____ is also a synonym for:

   - _____ signal; the information about the initial event that is the basis for subsequent modification of the event.
   - _____ loop; the causal path that leads from the initial generation of the _____ signal to the subsequent modification of the event.

   _____ is a mechanism, process or signal that is looped back to control a system within itself. Such a loop is called a _____ loop.

   a. Feedback
   b. 1990 Clean Air Act
   c. Feedback loop
   d. Positive feedback

5. _____ is a costing model that identifies activities in an organization and assigns the cost of each activity resource to all products and services according to the actual consumption by each: it assigns more indirect costs (overhead) into direct costs.

In this way an organization can establish the true cost of its individual products and services for the purposes of identifying and eliminating those which are unprofitable and lowering the prices of those which are overpriced.

In a business organization, the ABC methodology assigns an organization's resource costs through activities to the products and services provided to its customers.

   a. Activity-based costing
   c. A4e
   b. Indirect costs
   d. A Stake in the Outcome

6. In financial accounting, a _____ or statement of financial position is a summary of a person's or organization's balances. Assets, liabilities and ownership equity are listed as of a specific date, such as the end of its financial year. A _____ is often described as a snapshot of a company's financial condition.
   a. 1990 Clean Air Act
   c. Balance sheet
   b. 28-hour day
   d. 33 Strategies of War

7. In finance, a _____ or accounting ratio is a ratio of two selected numerical values taken from an enterprise's financial statements. There are many standard ratios used to try to evaluate the overall financial condition of a corporation or other organization. _____s may be used by managers within a firm, by current and potential shareholders (owners) of a firm, and by a firm's creditors.
   a. Rate of return
   c. Return on equity
   b. Financial ratio
   d. Return on sales

8. _____ are formal records of the financial activities of a business, person, or other entity. In British English, including United Kingdom company law, _____ are often referred to as accounts, although the term _____ is also used, particularly by accountants.

_____ provide an overview of a business or person's financial condition in both short and long term.

   a. Financial statements
   c. 33 Strategies of War
   b. 28-hour day
   d. 1990 Clean Air Act

9. In finance, _____ is borrowing money to supplement existing funds for investment in such a way that the potential positive or negative outcome is magnified and/or enhanced. It generally refers to using borrowed funds, or debt, so as to attempt to increase the returns to equity. Deleveraging is the action of reducing borrowings.
   a. Limited liability corporation
   c. Limited partners
   b. Private equity
   d. Gearing

10. Market _____ is a business, economics or investment term that refers to an asset's ability to be easily converted through an act of buying or selling without causing a significant movement in the price and with minimum loss of value. Money, or cash on hand, is the most liquid asset. An act of exchange of a less liquid asset with a more liquid asset is called liquidation.
   a. 28-hour day
   c. 33 Strategies of War
   b. 1990 Clean Air Act
   d. Liquidity

Chapter 16. Management Control

11. _____ is an idea in the field of Organizational studies and management which describes the psychology, attitudes, experiences, beliefs and Values (personal and cultural values) of an organization. It has been defined as 'the specific collection of values and norms that are shared by people and groups in an organization and that control the way they interact with each other and with stakeholders outside the organization.'

This definition continues to explain organizational values also known as 'beliefs and ideas about what kinds of goals members of an organization should pursue and ideas about the appropriate kinds or standards of behavior organizational members should use to achieve these goals. From organizational values develop organizational norms, guidelines or expectations that prescribe appropriate kinds of behavior by employees in particular situations and control the behavior of organizational members towards one another.'

_____ is not the same as corporate culture.

- a. Organizational development
- b. Organizational culture
- c. Organizational effectiveness
- d. Union shop

12. The _____ captures an expanded spectrum of values and criteria for measuring organizational success: economic, ecological and social. With the ratification of the United Nations and ICLEI _____ standard for urban and community accounting in early 2007, this became the dominant approach to public sector full cost accounting. Similar UN standards apply to natural capital and human capital measurement to assist in measurements required by _____, e.g. the ecoBudget standard for reporting ecological footprint.

- a. 1990 Clean Air Act
- b. 33 Strategies of War
- c. 28-hour day
- d. Triple bottom line

13. In engineering and manufacturing, _____ and quality engineering are used in developing systems to ensure products or services are designed and produced to meet or exceed customer requirements. Refer to the definition by Merriam-Webster for further information . These systems are often developed in conjunction with other business and engineering disciplines using a cross-functional approach.

- a. Process capability
- b. Single Minute Exchange of Die
- c. Statistical process control
- d. Quality control

Chapter 17. Operations Management

1. _____ is an area of business concerned with the production of goods and services, and involves the responsibility of ensuring that business operations are efficient in terms of using as little resource as needed, and effective in terms of meeting customer requirements. It is concerned with managing the process that converts inputs (in the forms of materials, labour and energy) into outputs (in the form of goods and services.)

Operations traditionally refers to the production of goods and services separately, although the distinction between these two main types of operations is increasingly difficult to make as manufacturers tend to merge product and service offerings.

a. AAAI
b. A4e
c. A Stake in the Outcome
d. Operations management

2. _____ is an organization's process of defining its strategy and making decisions on allocating its resources to pursue this strategy, including its capital and people. Various business analysis techniques can be used in _____, including SWOT analysis (Strengths, Weaknesses, Opportunities, and Threats) and PEST analysis (Political, Economic, Social, and Technological analysis) or STEER analysis involving Socio-cultural, Technological, Economic, Ecological, and Regulatory factors and EPISTEL (Environment, Political, Informatic, Social, Technological, Economic and Legal)

_____ is the formal consideration of an organization's future course. All _____ deals with at least one of three key questions:

1. 'What do we do?'
2. 'For whom do we do it?'
3. 'How do we excel?'

In business _____, the third question is better phrased 'How can we beat or avoid competition?'. (Bradford and Duncan, page 1.)

a. 28-hour day
b. 1990 Clean Air Act
c. 33 Strategies of War
d. Strategic planning

3. _____ is a software based production planning and inventory control system used to manage manufacturing processes. Although it is not common nowadays, it is possible to conduct _____ by hand as well.

An _____ system is intended to simultaneously meet three objectives:

- Ensure materials and products are available for production and delivery to customers.
- Maintain the lowest possible level of inventory.
- Plan manufacturing activities, delivery schedules and purchasing activities.

Manufacturing organizations, whatever their products, face the same daily practical problem - that customers want products to be available in a shorter time than it takes to make them. This means that some level of planning is required.

Chapter 17. Operations Management

a. 33 Strategies of War
c. 28-hour day
b. 1990 Clean Air Act
d. Material requirements planning

4. A _____ is a type of bar chart that illustrates a project schedule. _____s illustrate the start and finish dates of the terminal elements and summary elements of a project. Terminal elements and summary elements comprise the work breakdown structure of the project.
   a. 1990 Clean Air Act
   c. 28-hour day
   b. 33 Strategies of War
   d. Gantt chart

5. The Program (or Project) Evaluation and Review Technique, commonly abbreviated _____, is a model for project management designed to analyze and represent the tasks involved in completing a given project.

   _____ is a method to analyze the involved tasks in completing a given project, specially the time needed to complete each task, and identifying the minimum time needed to complete the total project.

   _____ was developed primarily to simplify the planning and scheduling of large and complex projects.

   a. 1990 Clean Air Act
   c. PERT
   b. 28-hour day
   d. 33 Strategies of War

6. A _____ system is a manufacturing system in which there is some amount of flexibility that allows the system to react in the case of changes, whether predicted or unpredicted. This flexibility is generally considered to fall into two categories, which both contain numerous subcategories.

   The first category, machine flexibility, covers the system's ability to be changed to produce new product types, and ability to change the order of operations executed on a part. The second category is called routing flexibility, which consists of the ability to use multiple machines to perform the same operation on a part, as well as the system's ability to absorb large-scale changes, such as in volume, capacity, or capability.

   a. Homeworkers
   c. Manufacturing resource planning
   b. Jidoka
   d. Flexible manufacturing

7. In economics, business, retail, and accounting, a _____ is the value of money that has been used up to produce something, and hence is not available for use anymore. In economics, a _____ is an alternative that is given up as a result of a decision. In business, the _____ may be one of acquisition, in which case the amount of money expended to acquire it is counted as _____.
   a. Fixed costs
   c. Cost allocation
   b. Cost overrun
   d. Cost

8. _____ is an effective method of monitoring a process through the use of control charts. Control charts enable the use of objective criteria for distinguishing background variation from events of significance based on statistical techniques. Much of its power lies in the ability to monitor both process center and its variation about that center.
   a. Process capability
   c. Statistical process control
   b. Single Minute Exchange of Die
   d. Quality control

Chapter 17. Operations Management

9. _____ is one of the managerial functions like planning, organizing, staffing and directing. It is an important function because it helps to check the errors and to take the corrective action so that deviation from standards are minimized and stated goals of the organization are achieved in desired manner. According to modern concepts, _____ is a foreseeing action whereas earlier concept of _____ was used only when errors were detected. _____ in management means setting standards, measuring actual performance and taking corrective action.

   a. Turnover
   b. Schedule of reinforcement
   c. Decision tree pruning
   d. Control

10. The term '_____' refers to the concept of collecting information and attempting to spot a pattern in the information. In some fields of study, the term '_____' has more formally-defined meanings.

    In project management _____ is a mathematical technique that uses historical results to predict future outcome.

    a. Least squares
    b. Stepwise regression
    c. Regression analysis
    d. Trend analysis

11. The _____ in statistical process control is a tool used to determine whether a manufacturing or business process is in a state of statistical control or not.

    If the chart indicates that the process is currently under control then it can be used with confidence to predict the future performance of the process. If the chart indicates that the process being monitored is not in control, the pattern it reveals can help determine the source of variation to be eliminated to bring the process back into control.

    a. Simple moving average
    b. Time series analysis
    c. Failure rate
    d. Control chart

12. _____ is a statistical technique in decision making that is used for selection of a limited number of tasks that produce significant overall effect. It uses the Pareto principle - the idea that by doing 20% of work you can generate 80% of the advantage of doing the entire job. Or in terms of quality improvement, a large majority of problems (80%) are produced by a few key causes (20%.)

    a. Polychoric correlation
    b. Goodness of fit
    c. Probability matching
    d. Pareto analysis

13. The _____ is a measurable property of a process to the specification, expressed as a _____ index (e.g., C_{pk} or C_{pm}) or as a process performance index (e.g., P_{pk} or P_{pm}.) The output of this measurement is usually illustrated by a histogram and calculations that predict how many parts will be produced out of specification.

    _____ is also defined as the capability of a process to meet its purpose as managed by an organization's management and process definition structures ISO 15504.

    a. Quality control
    b. Single Minute Exchange of Die
    c. Statistical process control
    d. Process capability

Chapter 17. Operations Management

14. _____ refers to metrics and measures of output from production processes, per unit of input. Labor _____, for example, is typically measured as a ratio of output per labor-hour, an input. _____ may be conceived of as a metrics of the technical or engineering efficiency of production.
    a. Master production schedule
    b. Productivity
    c. Value engineering
    d. Remanufacturing

15. In economics, _____ (TFP) is a variable which accounts for effects in total output not caused by inputs. For example, a year with unusually good weather will tend to have higher output, because bad weather hinders agricultural output. A variable like weather does not directly relate to unit inputs, so weather is considered a _____ variable.
    a. Strict liability
    b. Collaborative Planning, Forecasting and Replenishment
    c. Total-factor productivity
    d. Minimax

16. _____ can be considered to have three main components: quality control, quality assurance and quality improvement. _____ is focused not only on product quality, but also the means to achieve it. _____ therefore uses quality assurance and control of processes as well as products to achieve more consistent quality.
    a. 28-hour day
    b. 1990 Clean Air Act
    c. Total quality management
    d. Quality management

17. _____ ('Plan-Do-Check-Act') is an iterative four-step problem-solving process typically used in business process improvement. It is also known as the Deming Cycle, Shewhart cycle, Deming Wheel, or Plan-Do-Study-Act.

    _____ was made popular by Dr. W. Edwards Deming, who is considered by many to be the father of modern quality control; however it was always referred to by him as the Shewhart cycle. Later in Deming's career, he modified _____ to Plan, Do, Study, Act (PDSA) so as to better describe his recommendations.

    a. Decentralization
    b. Management by exception
    c. Management team
    d. PDCA

18. A _____ is a volunteer group composed of workers (or even students), usually under the leadership of their supervisor (but they can elect a team leader), who are trained to identify, analyse and solve work-related problems and present their solutions to management in order to improve the performance of the organization, and motivate and enrich the work of employees. When matured, true _____s become self-managing, having gained the confidence of management.
    _____s are an alternative to the dehumanising concept of the Division of Labour, where workers or individuals are treated like robots.
    a. Quality circle
    b. Competency-based job descriptions
    c. Certified in Production and Inventory Management
    d. Connectionist expert systems

19. _____ is a business management strategy aimed at embedding awareness of quality in all organizational processes. _____ has been widely used in manufacturing, education, hospitals, call centers, government, and service industries, as well as NASA space and science programs.

As defined by the International Organization for Standardization (ISO):

'_____ is a management approach for an organization, centered on quality, based on the participation of all its members and aiming at long-term success through customer satisfaction, and benefits to all members of the organization and to society.' ISO 8402:1994

One major aim is to reduce variation from every process so that greater consistency of effort is obtained. (Royse, D., Thyer, B., Padgett D., ' Logan T., 2006)

   a. Total quality management
   b. 28-hour day
   c. Quality management
   d. 1990 Clean Air Act

20. The _____, widely known as ISO, is an international-standard-setting body composed of representatives from various national standards organizations. Founded on 23 February 1947, the organization promulgates worldwide proprietary industrial and commercial standards. It is headquartered in Geneva, Switzerland.
   a. A4e
   b. A Stake in the Outcome
   c. AAAI
   d. International Organization for Standardization

21. _____ is a family of standards for quality management systems. _____ is maintained by ISO, the International Organization for Standardization and is administered by accreditation and certification bodies. The rules are updated, the time and changes in the requirements for quality, motivate change.
   a. AAAI
   b. A Stake in the Outcome
   c. A4e
   d. ISO 9000

22. _____ is a Japanese philosophy that focuses on continuous improvement throughout all aspects of life. When applied to the workplace, _____ activities continually improve all functions of a business, from manufacturing to management and from the CEO to the assembly line workers. By improving standardized activities and processes, _____ aims to eliminate waste.
   a. Psychological pricing
   b. Sensitivity analysis
   c. Kaizen
   d. Cross-docking

23. _____ is a concept related to lean and just-in-time (JIT) production. The Japanese word _____ is a common term meaning 'signboard' or 'billboard'. According to Taiichi Ohno, the man credited with developing JIT, _____ is a means through which JIT is achieved.
   a. Kanban
   b. Trademark
   c. Risk management
   d. Succession planning

24. _____ is an inventory strategy that strives to improve the return on investment of a business by reducing in-process inventory and its associated carrying costs. To meet _____ objectives, the process relies on signals between different points in the process. This means the process is often driven by a series of signals, or Kanban, which tell production when to make the next part. Kanban are usually 'tickets' but can be simple visual signals, such as the presence or absence of a part on a shelf. Implemented correctly, _____ can dramatically improve a manufacturing organization's return on investment, quality, and efficiency.

Chapter 17. Operations Management

a. 33 Strategies of War
c. 1990 Clean Air Act
b. 28-hour day
d. Just-in-time

25. _____ is a company-wide computer software system used to manage and coordinate all the resources, information, and functions of a business from shared data stores.

An _____ system has a service-oriented architecture with modular hardware and software units and 'services' that communicate on a local area network. The modular design allows a business to add or reconfigure modules (perhaps from different vendors) while preserving data integrity in one shared database that may be centralized or distributed.

a. AAAI
c. A4e
b. A Stake in the Outcome
d. Enterprise resource planning

Chapter 18. Managing Information System

1. _____ is one of the managerial functions like planning, organizing, staffing and directing. It is an important function because it helps to check the errors and to take the corrective action so that deviation from standards are minimized and stated goals of the organization are achieved in desired manner. According to modern concepts, _____ is a foreseeing action whereas earlier concept of _____ was used only when errors were detected. _____ in management means setting standards, measuring actual performance and taking corrective action.
   a. Decision tree pruning
   b. Schedule of reinforcement
   c. Turnover
   d. Control

2. _____ is the process of extracting hidden patterns from data. As more data is gathered, with the amount of data doubling every three years, _____ is becoming an increasingly important tool to transform this data into information. It is commonly used in a wide range of profiling practices, such as marketing, surveillance, fraud detection and scientific discovery.
   a. 1990 Clean Air Act
   b. Decision tree learning
   c. 28-hour day
   d. Data mining

3. A _____ is a commercial building for storage of goods. _____s are used by manufacturers, importers, exporters, wholesalers, transport businesses, customs, etc. They are usually large plain buildings in industrial areas of cities and towns.
   a. 1990 Clean Air Act
   b. 28-hour day
   c. 33 Strategies of War
   d. Warehouse

4. A _____ is a list of the general tasks and responsibilities of a position. Typically, it also includes to whom the position reports, specifications such as the qualifications needed by the person in the job, salary range for the position, etc. A _____ is usually developed by conducting a job analysis, which includes examining the tasks and sequences of tasks necessary to perform the job.
   a. Recruitment Process Insourcing
   b. Recruitment advertising
   c. Recruitment
   d. Job description

5. _____, commonly referred to as 'eBusiness' or 'e-Business', may be defined as the utilization of information and communication technologies (ICT) in support of all the activities of business. Commerce constitutes the exchange of products and services between businesses, groups and individuals and hence can be seen as one of the essential activities of any business. Hence, electronic commerce or eCommerce focuses on the use of ICT to enable the external activities and relationships of the business with individuals, groups and other businesses.
   a. Electronic business
   b. A Stake in the Outcome
   c. AAAI
   d. A4e

6. An _____ is a private network that uses Internet protocols, network connectivity, and possibly the public telecommunication system to securely share part of an organization's information or operations with suppliers, vendors, partners, customers or other businesses. An _____ can be viewed as part of a company's intranet that is extended to users outside the company (e.g.: normally over the Internet.) It has also been described as a 'state of mind' in which the Internet is perceived as a way to do business with a preapproved set of other companies business-to-business (B2B), in isolation from all other Internet users.
   a. AAAI
   b. A4e
   c. Extranet
   d. A Stake in the Outcome

Chapter 18. Managing Information System

7. _____ is the intelligence of machines and the branch of computer science which aims to create it. Major _____ textbooks define the field as 'the study and design of intelligent agents,' where an intelligent agent is a system that perceives its environment and takes actions which maximize its chances of success. John McCarthy, who coined the term in 1956, defines it as 'the science and engineering of making intelligent machines.'

The field was founded on the claim that a central property of human beings, intelligence--the sapience of Homo sapiens--can be so precisely described that it can be simulated by a machine.

- a. A Stake in the Outcome
- b. Artificial intelligence
- c. A4e
- d. AAAI

8. _____ is a form of applied ethics that examines ethical principles and moral or ethical problems that arise in a business environment. It applies to all aspects of business conduct and is relevant to the conduct of individuals and business organizations as a whole. Applied ethics is a field of ethics that deals with ethical questions in many fields such as medical, technical, legal and _____.

- a. Corporate Sustainability
- b. Hypernorms
- c. Facilitation payments
- d. Business ethics

9. _____ is a company-wide computer software system used to manage and coordinate all the resources, information, and functions of a business from shared data stores.

An _____ system has a service-oriented architecture with modular hardware and software units and 'services' that communicate on a local area network. The modular design allows a business to add or reconfigure modules (perhaps from different vendors) while preserving data integrity in one shared database that may be centralized or distributed.

- a. A4e
- b. Enterprise resource planning
- c. AAAI
- d. A Stake in the Outcome

10. _____ is a concept in ethics with several meanings. It is often used synonymously with such concepts as responsibility, answerability, enforcement, blameworthiness, liability and other terms associated with the expectation of account-giving. As an aspect of governance, it has been central to discussions related to problems in both the public and private (corporation) worlds.

- a. A Stake in the Outcome
- b. A4e
- c. Accountability
- d. Usury

11. _____ constitute a class of computer-based information systems including knowledge-based systems that support decision-making activities.

_____ are a specific class of computerized information systems that supports business and organizational decision-making activities. A properly-designed _____ is an interactive software-based system intended to help decision makers compile useful information from raw data, documents, personal knowledge, and/or business models to identify and solve problems and make decisions.

a. 1990 Clean Air Act
b. 28-hour day
c. Spatial Decision Support Systems
d. Decision support systems

12. An _____ is software that attempts to reproduce the performance of one or more human experts, most commonly in a specific problem domain, and is a traditional application and/or subfield of artificial intelligence. A wide variety of methods can be used to simulate the performance of the expert however common to most or all are 1) the creation of a so-called 'knowledgebase' which uses some knowledge representation formalism to capture the Subject Matter Experts (SME) knowledge and 2) a process of gathering that knowledge from the SME and codifying it according to the formalism, which is called knowledge engineering. _____s may or may not have learning components but a third common element is that once the system is developed it is proven by being placed in the same real world problem solving situation as the human SME, typically as an aid to human workers or a supplement to some information system.
a. A Stake in the Outcome
b. Expert system
c. A4e
d. AAAI

13. _____ is the use of control systems (such as numerical control, programmable logic control, and other industrial control systems), in concert with other applications of information technology (such as computer-aided technologies [CAD, CAM, CAx]), to control industrial machinery and processes, reducing the need for human intervention. In the scope of industrialization, _____ is a step beyond mechanization. Whereas mechanization provided human operators with machinery to assist them with the physical requirements of work, _____ greatly reduces the need for human sensory and mental requirements as well.
a. A Stake in the Outcome
b. A4e
c. AAAI
d. Automation

14. A _____ is a subset of the overall internal controls of a business covering the application of people, documents, technologies, and procedures by management accountants to solving business problems such as costing a product, service or a business-wide strategy. _____s are distinct from regular information systems in that they are used to analyze other information systems applied in operational activities in the organization. Academically, the term is commonly used to refer to the group of information management methods tied to the automation or support of human decision making, e.g. Decision Support Systems, Expert systems, and Executive information systems.
a. 28-hour day
b. 1990 Clean Air Act
c. Strategic information system
d. Management Information system

15. _____ consists of the processes a company uses to track and organize its contacts with its current and prospective customers. _____ software is used to support these processes; information about customers and customer interactions can be entered, stored and accessed by employees in different company departments. Typical _____ goals are to improve services provided to customers, and to use customer contact information for targeted marketing.
a. Disruptive technology
b. Customer relationship management
c. Marketing plan
d. Green marketing

16. An _____ is a type of management information system intended to facilitate and support the information and decision-making needs of senior executives by providing easy access to both internal and external information relevant to meeting the strategic goals of the organization. It is commonly considered as a specialized form of a Decision Support System (DSS)

Chapter 18. Managing Information System

The emphasis of _____ is on graphical displays and easy-to-use user interfaces. They offer strong reporting and drill-down capabilities.

a. A4e
b. A Stake in the Outcome
c. AAAI
d. Executive information system

17. _____ is, in very basic words, a position a firm occupies against its competitors.

According to Michael Porter, the three methods for creating a sustainable _____ are through:

1. Cost leadership

2. Differentiation

3. Focus (economics)

a. 1990 Clean Air Act
b. 28-hour day
c. Theory Z
d. Competitive advantage

18. _____, commonly known as e-commerce, consists of the buying and selling of products or services over electronic systems such as the Internet and other computer networks. The amount of trade conducted electronically has grown extraordinarily with widespread Internet usage. The use of commerce is conducted in this way, spurring and drawing on innovations in electronic funds transfer, supply chain management, Internet marketing, online transaction processing, electronic data interchange (EDI), inventory management systems, and automated data collection systems.

a. Online shopping
b. A Stake in the Outcome
c. A4e
d. Electronic Commerce

19. The _____ of an edge is $c_f(u, v) = c(u, v) - f(u, v)$. This defines a residual network denoted $G_f(V, \overline{E_f})$, giving the amount of available capacity. See that there can be an edge from u to v in the residual network, even though there is no edge from u to v in the original network.

a. 28-hour day
b. 33 Strategies of War
c. 1990 Clean Air Act
d. Residual capacity

20. _____ is a system of training a new generation of practitioners of a skill. Apprentices (or in early modern usage 'prentices') or prot>ég>és build their careers from _____s. Most of their training is done on the job while working for an employer who helps the apprentices learn their trade, in exchange for their continuing labour for an agreed period after they become skilled.

a. A4e
b. AAAI
c. A Stake in the Outcome
d. Apprenticeship

21. The _____ in statistical process control is a tool used to determine whether a manufacturing or business process is in a state of statistical control or not.

If the chart indicates that the process is currently under control then it can be used with confidence to predict the future performance of the process. If the chart indicates that the process being monitored is not in control, the pattern it reveals can help determine the source of variation to be eliminated to bring the process back into control.

a. Control chart
b. Failure rate
c. Simple moving average
d. Time series analysis

22. _____ is the level of inventory that minimizes the total inventory holding costs and ordering costs. The framework used to determine this order quantity is also known as Wilson _____ Model. The model was developed by F. W. Harris in 1913.

a. Economic order quantity
b. Effective executive
c. Event management
d. Anti-leadership

23. _____ is the principle that in open systems a given end state can be reached by many potential means. The term is due to Ludwig von Bertalanffy, the founder of General Systems Theory. He prefers this term, in contrast to 'goal', in describing complex systems' similar or convergent behavior.

a. A4e
b. AAAI
c. A Stake in the Outcome
d. Equifinality

24. In finance, a _____ or accounting ratio is a ratio of two selected numerical values taken from an enterprise's financial statements. There are many standard ratios used to try to evaluate the overall financial condition of a corporation or other organization. _____s may be used by managers within a firm, by current and potential shareholders (owners) of a firm, and by a firm's creditors.

a. Financial ratio
b. Rate of return
c. Return on sales
d. Return on equity

25. _____ involves establishing specific, measurable and time-targeted objectives. Work on the theory of goal-setting suggests that it's an effective tool for making progress by ensuring that participants in a group with a common goal are clearly aware of what is expected from them if an objective is to be achieved. On a personal level, setting goals is a process that allows people to specify then work towards their own objectives - most commonly with financial or career-based goals.

a. Digital strategy
b. Resource-based view
c. Catfish effect
d. Goal setting

26. _____ is the strategic and coherent approach to the management of an organisation's most valued assets - the people working there who individually and collectively contribute to the achievement of the objectives of the business. The terms '_____' and 'human resources' (HR) have largely replaced the term 'personnel management' as a description of the processes involved in managing people in organizations. In simple sense, _____ means employing people, developing their resources, utilizing, maintaining and compensating their services in tune with the job and organizational requirement.

a. Job knowledge
b. Revolving door syndrome
c. Progressive discipline
d. Human resource management

27. _____ is a term defined by the Oxford English Dictionary as an individual's 'course or progress through life '. It is usually considered to pertain to remunerative work (and sometimes also formal education.)

The etymology of the term is somewhat ironic in that it comes from the Latin word carrera, which means race .

a. Nursing shortage
c. Spatial mismatch
b. Career planning
d. Career

28. In organizational development (or OD), the study of _____ looks at:

- how individuals manage their careers within and between organizations
- and how organizations structure the career progress of their members, it can also be tied into succession planning within some organizations.

In personal development, _____ is:

- ' ... the total constellation of psychological, sociological, educational, physical, economic, and chance factors that combine to influence the nature and significance of work in the total lifespan of any given individual.'

- '... the lifelong psychological and behavioral processes as well as contextual influences shaping one's career over the life span. As such, _____ involves the person's creation of a career pattern, decision-making style, integration of life roles, values expression, and life-role self concepts.'

Figures in _____

- Jeff A. Brown
- Jesse B. Davis
- Caela Farren
- John L. Holland
- Kris Magnusson
- Frank Parsons
- Vance Peavy
- Edgar Schein
- Rino Schreuder
- Mark L. Savickas
- Donald Super

a. Sole proprietorship
c. Career development
b. Horizontal integration
d. Business process reengineering

Chapter 18. Managing Information System

29. _____ is a process of planning and controlling the performance or execution of any type of activity, such as:

- a project (project _____) or
- a process (process _____, sometimes referred to as the process performance measurement and management system.)

Organization's senior management is responsible for carrying out its _____.

a. Management process
c. Participatory management
b. Work design
d. Human Relations Movement

30. _____ is a method by which the job performance of an employee is evaluated _____ is a part of career development.

_____s are regular reviews of employee performance within organizations

Generally, the aims of a _____ are to:

- Give feedback on performance to employees.
- Identify employee training needs.
- Document criteria used to allocate organizational rewards.
- Form a basis for personnel decisions: salary increases, promotions, disciplinary actions, etc.
- Provide the opportunity for organizational diagnosis and development.
- Facilitate communication between employee and administraton
- Validate selection techniques and human resource policies to meet federal Equal Employment Opportunity requirements.

A common approach to assessing performance is to use a numerical or scalar rating system whereby managers are asked to score an individual against a number of objectives/attributes. In some companies, employees receive assessments from their manager, peers, subordinates and customers while also performing a self assessment.

a. Performance appraisal
c. Personnel management
b. Human resource management
d. Progressive discipline

31. _____ is a term originating in military organization theory, but now used more commonly in business management, particularly human resource management. _____ refers to the number of subordinates a supervisor has.

In the hierarchical business organization of the past it was not uncommon to see average spans of 1 to 10 or even less. That is, one manager supervised ten employees on average.

a. Mentoring
c. CIFMS
b. Span of control
d. Senior management

Chapter 18. Managing Information System

32. _____ according to Onuoha (2007) is the practice of starting new organizations or revitalizing mature organizations, particularly new businesses generally in response to identified opportunities. _____ is often a difficult undertaking, as a vast majority of new businesses fail. Entrepreneurial activities are substantially different depending on the type of organization that is being started.
   a. AAAI
   b. Entrepreneurship
   c. A Stake in the Outcome
   d. A4e

33. A _____ is a business that is privately owned and operated, with a small number of employees and relatively low volume of sales. The legal definition of 'small' often varies by country and industry, but is generally under 100 employees in the United States and under 50 employees in the European Union. In comparison, the definition of mid-sized business by the number of employees is generally under 500 in the U.S. and 250 for the European Union.
   a. Pre-determined overhead rate
   b. Critical Success Factor
   c. Small business
   d. Golden Boot Compensation

34. An _____ is a person who has possession of an enterprise and assumes significant accountability for the inherent risks and the outcome. It is an ambitious leader who combines land, labor, and capital to create and market new goods or services. The term is a loanword from French and was first defined by the Irish economist Richard Cantillon.
   a. Entrepreneur
   b. AAAI
   c. A Stake in the Outcome
   d. A4e

35. _____ is a business management strategy aimed at embedding awareness of quality in all organizational processes. _____ has been widely used in manufacturing, education, hospitals, call centers, government, and service industries, as well as NASA space and science programs.

As defined by the International Organization for Standardization (ISO):

> '_____ is a management approach for an organization, centered on quality, based on the participation of all its members and aiming at long-term success through customer satisfaction, and benefits to all members of the organization and to society.' ISO 8402:1994

One major aim is to reduce variation from every process so that greater consistency of effort is obtained. (Royse, D., Thyer, B., Padgett D., ' Logan T., 2006)

   a. Quality management
   b. Total quality management
   c. 28-hour day
   d. 1990 Clean Air Act

36. _____ can be considered to have three main components: quality control, quality assurance and quality improvement. _____ is focused not only on product quality, but also the means to achieve it. _____ therefore uses quality assurance and control of processes as well as products to achieve more consistent quality.
   a. 1990 Clean Air Act
   b. 28-hour day
   c. Total quality management
   d. Quality management

Chapter 1

1. d	2. d	3. c	4. d	5. c	6. d	7. a	8. a	9. d	10. b
11. d	12. d	13. d	14. d	15. d	16. a	17. c	18. d	19. d	20. d
21. d	22. a	23. b	24. d	25. a	26. b	27. c	28. d	29. d	30. c
31. d	32. d	33. c	34. d	35. d	36. a	37. d	38. c	39. c	40. c
41. d	42. d	43. d	44. d	45. d	46. b	47. d	48. c	49. c	50. b
51. d	52. d	53. d							

Chapter 2

1. d	2. c	3. b	4. d	5. b	6. c	7. c	8. a	9. b	10. c
11. b	12. a	13. d	14. d	15. d	16. a	17. a	18. d	19. b	20. d
21. b	22. d	23. d	24. d	25. d	26. a	27. c	28. a	29. d	30. a
31. c	32. c	33. d	34. c	35. c	36. d	37. d	38. d	39. d	40. c
41. a	42. d	43. d							

Chapter 3

1. a	2. b	3. d	4. a	5. a	6. d	7. b	8. b	9. c	10. c
11. c	12. c	13. d	14. d	15. a	16. a	17. a	18. d	19. b	20. d
21. d									

Chapter 4

1. d	2. d	3. d	4. c	5. d	6. c	7. d	8. d	9. d	10. d
11. d	12. c	13. c	14. d	15. d					

Chapter 5

1. a	2. d	3. d	4. d	5. b	6. d	7. c	8. d	9. d	10. d
11. d	12. d	13. a	14. d	15. d	16. c				

Chapter 6

1. d	2. d	3. d	4. c	5. a	6. a	7. d	8. d	9. d	10. a
11. c	12. b	13. a	14. a	15. d	16. d	17. d	18. c	19. a	20. d

Chapter 7

1. b	2. d	3. b	4. d	5. d	6. d	7. d	8. a	9. d	10. d
11. a	12. a	13. c	14. d	15. d	16. b	17. b	18. c	19. a	20. d
21. d	22. a	23. c	24. b	25. d	26. c	27. b	28. c	29. d	30. b
31. a	32. a								

Chapter 8

1. d	2. b	3. a	4. d	5. a	6. d	7. d	8. d	9. a	10. a
11. d	12. d	13. a	14. c	15. d	16. d	17. d	18. d	19. d	20. b
21. d	22. b	23. d	24. d	25. d	26. b	27. d	28. c		

ANSWER KEY

Chapter 9
1. d	2. d	3. b	4. d	5. d	6. a	7. b	8. b	9. d	10. c
11. d	12. b	13. b	14. d	15. d	16. d	17. d	18. d	19. d	20. d
21. d	22. b	23. b	24. c	25. b	26. d				

Chapter 10
1. c	2. d	3. b	4. d	5. d	6. d	7. a	8. d	9. d	10. d
11. b	12. c	13. d	14. d	15. d	16. d	17. a	18. a	19. d	20. a
21. c	22. d	23. d	24. d	25. c	26. d	27. b	28. a	29. a	30. a
31. d	32. d	33. b	34. b	35. a	36. b	37. a	38. a	39. a	40. b
41. d	42. b	43. a	44. b	45. c	46. c	47. d	48. b	49. d	50. d
51. c	52. a	53. d	54. a	55. a	56. a	57. d	58. d	59. d	60. d

Chapter 11
1. b	2. b	3. b	4. b	5. d	6. a	7. d	8. d	9. d	10. d
11. c	12. c	13. b	14. b	15. c	16. c	17. c	18. d	19. d	20. b
21. d	22. d	23. c	24. d	25. b	26. d	27. a	28. b	29. c	30. d

Chapter 12
1. d	2. d	3. b	4. b	5. c	6. d	7. d	8. a	9. d	10. d
11. d	12. d	13. b	14. b	15. c	16. c	17. b	18. a	19. c	20. d
21. d									

Chapter 13
1. d	2. b	3. a	4. c	5. a	6. a	7. c	8. c	9. d	10. b
11. d	12. d								

Chapter 14
1. d	2. b	3. b	4. a	5. b	6. b	7. d	8. a	9. a	10. d
11. d	12. d	13. d	14. d	15. d					

Chapter 15
1. d	2. c	3. d	4. b	5. b	6. d	7. b	8. b	9. d	10. c

Chapter 16
1. c	2. a	3. d	4. a	5. a	6. c	7. b	8. a	9. d	10. d
11. b	12. d	13. d							

Chapter 17
1. d	2. d	3. d	4. d	5. c	6. d	7. d	8. c	9. d	10. d
11. d	12. d	13. d	14. b	15. c	16. d	17. d	18. a	19. a	20. d
21. d	22. c	23. a	24. d	25. d					

Chapter 18

1. d	2. d	3. d	4. d	5. a	6. c	7. b	8. d	9. b	10. c
11. d	12. b	13. d	14. d	15. b	16. d	17. d	18. d	19. d	20. d
21. a	22. a	23. d	24. a	25. d	26. d	27. d	28. c	29. a	30. a
31. b	32. b	33. c	34. a	35. b	36. d				

www.ingramcontent.com/pod-product-compliance
Lightning Source LLC
Chambersburg PA
CBHW082050230426
43670CB00016B/2844